CHAMPAGNE
ON A BUDGET

ROSTERS LTD.

About the Author

Patrick Delaforce was educated at Winchester, served as a troop Commander from Normandy to the Baltic in the 1939/1945 War. Became a Port Wine Shipper in Portugal, and also worked in New York and the City of London.

He recently returned to Brighton after seven years as a vineyard owner in France and is now fully occupied as an author. Among his recent writing are books on historical research, French regional wines and Lady Frances 'Fanny' Nelson.

Other Rosters books by Patrick Delaforce:–
- French Riviera on a Budget
- Gascony and Armagnac on a Budget
- The French Riviera

CHAMPAGNE ON A BUDGET

PATRICK DELAFORCE

ROSTERS LTD.

Published by ROSTERS LTD.
60 Welbeck Street, London W1
© Rosters Ltd.
ISBN 0 948032 33 2

First Edition 1989

Designed and published by ROSTERS
Typeset by Lovell Baines Print Ltd, Newbury, Berkshire.
Printed and bound in Great Britain by Cox & Wyman Ltd,
Reading, Berkshire.

Pictures courtesy of the French Government Tourist Office.

CONTENTS

Champagne vineyards: pickers at work

CHAPTER ONE:
YOUR PICK OF CHAMPAGNE TREATS

It is curious that the great wine writers have written over the centuries about the famous, perhaps the most famous, wine in the world – champagne – however, those same authors have failed to write in detail about the people and the area in which it is grown.

Getting there

The Champagne region is 90 miles (144 km) north east of Paris and easily reached via Laon, Soissons or Chateau Thierry from the west, or via Chalons sur Marne from the south east. Trips by train, plane, bus or car are equally easy. So there is no excuse for not going to Champagne!

The area actually consists of three departements. The largest is La Marne with a population of 550,000 and a land area of 8,200 sq. km. Here Reims (pronounced in a variety of ways including rinss, rans or reems) is the main city and the centre of the Champagne wine business. To the south is the departement of the Aube, rather smaller, with a population of 300,000 and land area of 6,000 sq. km. Finally there is the Haute Marne, slightly south east, equally small with a population of 210,000 and a land area of 6,200 sq. km.

Regional highlights

The most obvious reason to go to Champagne is to visit some or all of the great champagne houses, see how their wines are grown, made and stored and then taste them! As there are 52 shippers this will take some time but will be highly enjoyable.

A survey in depth will take a year! The local cuisine is good and complements the wine. In this book I will show you where to stay economically and where the good value little restaurants are to be found. I have also identified 60 or 70 small towns and villages which I think worth a visit!

Of course, the area has much more to offer than simply a splendid wine holiday. It featured as much in history books as almost any area of France. Charlemagne, Joan of Arc, Napoleon, and two recent World Wars, have left their traces. So too has General de Gaulle, who lived and died in Champagne country.

The architectural wonders include cathedrals, abbeys, chateaux and many fine museums. Some of the towns are absolute gems and I would single out Troyes and Langres as being well worth a visit as well as, of course, Reims and Chalons sur Marne.

For lovers of the great outdoors there are two major nature reserves, the Forest of Orient Park in the Aube and the Montagne de Reims in the Marne. There are also two animal reserves where wild boar, bear (yes, truly), stags, roe and fallow deer can be seen, plus wild sheep! There are half a dozen good-sized lakes where you can sail, swim, water-ski, row or fish — ideal for the family holiday. There are hundreds of kilometres of rivers and canals for water-based holidays. None of these delights need cost you a fortune. Quite a few English tour companies offer a holiday at reasonable prices and these are listed in Chapter Three.

View of the countryside

The Champagne countryside is at its best in the spring and autumn, but fiendishly busy around vintage time. The climate is the same as in the south of England — distinctly chilly in winter, less rainfall and rather warmer in mid-summer. The low rolling hills, shallow green valleys and the slow-moving silver rivers have a quiet charm. All the wine villages have grey steepled churches, the cornfields have cornflowers and poppies on the verges, and the yellow mustard fields blend their finished product with the local wine of Magenta (suburb of Epernay) to produce 'moutarde au vin provenant de la Champagne'. All the vines are attached with metal supports — bare, cold and lonely in the winter, and in full leaf red, bronzed and gold in the autumn.

So think of yourself being in chalky Kent and Sussex but with several differences — huge, wide-open landscapes — space everywhere (very little urban clutter or ribbon development) and the incomparable wine 'partout'. Remember too, we left the flower of our young men slaughtered in World War I and buried in a dozen military cemeteries, mainly west south west and close to Reims (see Chapter Nine).

In this book 'Champagne on a Budget' I hope to encourage the independent traveller to discover the hidden beauty of one of the world's greatest wine regions. In each of the chapters devoted to the three departements you will find full details of dozens of small modest hotels and restaurants — many of them off the beaten track. Hotels where a room (for two people) will cost about 100 francs for the night and where you can enjoy an excellent three or four course meal at about 50 francs per head if you choose the prix fixe menu. Allowing for breakfast at 15–18 francs per head and a picnic lunch purchased in a supermarché, the budget for two people per day should not exceed 400 francs, including petrol and chateaux/museum charges. If your body tires of a rich diet of food and wine then a visit to the spa town of Bourbonne les Bains in the east of the region, where the citizens and soldiers of the pre-Roman times sought a cure, will restore your spirits. So put the Champagne area on your holiday menu for next year. The countryside of joie de vivre.

As in previous books in this series I have written separate chapters on:—

> —Interesting towns and villages
> —Historic buildings and museums
> —Accommodation
> —Food and restaurants

I hope this will help you select the information you need more easily than if the guide was produced totally on a geographic basis. For towns of any size I have given the population figure. I think it helps to know if Sezanne has 6,000 or 60,000 population before you visit it — it helps put the scale of what you are about to see in proportion!

Some of the main events in Champagne

January — Fête de la Saint Vincent, patron of vignerons, usually on the 22nd in most of the wine villages around Epernay, Bar sur Aube and Ambonnay. Pilgrimage of St. Remi in Reims.

March — Carnival festivities in Reims and Chalons sur Marne.

Spring — Good Friday fairs in Les Riceys and Troyes.

May — Major pilgrimage to Notre Dame de l'Epine — the famous basilica.
Fête du muguet (lilies of the valley) in Chaource (Aube).
Fête of Joan of Arc (4th Sunday) in Reims.
International Folklore Festival Chalons sur Marne and Ste. Marie du Lac (near Vitry).

June — The Champagne Fair in Troyes.
Musical spring festival at Notre Dame de l'Epine.

June-October — Popular festival of champagne in Troyes.

September — Cider festival in the Pays d'Othe (west of Troyes).
The honey market at Verzy, near Epernay.
Pilgrimage in Bar sur Seine.
Wine fair in Bar sur Aube.
Cauliflower fête at Brienne le Chateau (Aube).

October — Cheese fair at Chaource (Aube).
First week — pilgrimage of St. Remi in Reims.

Christmas Day — The Christmas Shepherds fête at Braux Ste. Cohière.

Historic buildings

The most interesting chateaux and castles cover a wide range of styles — fortified and defensive, classical and sober or refined and Regency in style. They are not in the same class architecturally as those splendours on the Loire, but each one listed is worth a visit.

a)   Chateaux and castles

Marne
Boursault; Brugny Vaudancourt; Braux Ste Cohière; Dormans; Esternay; Montmortlucy; Reveillon and St Martin d'Ablois.

Aube
Arcis sur Aube; Barberey St Sulpice; Brienne le Chateau; Isle Aumont; Domaine de Menois; La Motte Tilly; Mussy sur Seine; Rumilly les Vaudes and Ville Mereuil.

Haute Marne
Cirey sur Blaise; Dinteville; Joinville; Langres; Le Pailly; Parnot; Prangey.

The great cathedrals, abbeys and churches are so many that the choice has to be rather arbitrary.

b)   Abbeys

Marne
Hautvillers; Igny; Le Reclus (Montmortlucy); St Remi basilique (Reims) and Trois Fontaines (Sermaize les Bains).

Aube
Le Paraclet (Nogent sur Seine) and Clairvaux.

Haute Marne
Auberive and Morimond.

c)   Cathedrals

Marne
Reims; Chalons sur Marne; L'Epine (basilique).

CHAMPAGNE ON A BUDGET

Aube
Troyes.

Haute Marne
Langres.

Travel checklist

Obviously make sure your passport is valid and up to date, your favourite ferry company is not on strike and your tickets are accurate (right days and times and destinations). You will, I hope, have not only purchased a Green Card for your car but have obtained truly comprehensive insurance for all travellers accompanying you. Far better to spend a few more pounds and if anything over-insure your family and all belongings. Selecting cash, credit cards, Eurocheques, travellers cheques or what have you has so many pros and cons. I am a Eurocheque fan, but other people swear by Visa, Access or Barclaycards. The Michelin maps you need are Nos. 56, 61, 62 and 66 and can easily be purchased in the UK. Bring some soap too as many modest French hotels are reluctant to provide any!

The choice of route is usually between the fast autoroutes (all 'péage' i.e. quite expensive tolls) but naturally very quick, and the more direct 'route nationale' or local roads, which are cheaper, usually much more interesting but may need map-reading through the towns on the way. It depends on time available for the journey, whether there are any interesting detours en route and the map reading skills of your family. Whatever you do, keep away from the Paris périphéric ring road in the four rush-hour periods 8.00 a.m.–9.00 a.m., 11.45 a.m.–12.15 p.m. (lunch time), 1.45 p.m.–2.15 p.m. (return from lunch) and 6.00 p.m.–7.00 p.m. (office closing times).

Hotel bookings

Our family tend to make a telephone reservation for the first night of the holiday — a few days in advance, giving us some leeway for arrival. Aim to arrive before 8.00 p.m. as Madame will be getting apprehensive in her kitchen if you are any later. Many provincial restaurants serve the evening meal from 7.00 p.m. (and lunch from noon).

Hotel rooms are priced per room irrespective of whether it is for one or two people. The price is posted in the entrance lobby and behind the room door. Madame will endeavour to offer you the most expensive room she has not yet 'sold' for the night. Be firm, look at the room list and ask for a room to suit your budget and then ask to see it before making a decision. This is normal practice and Madame will expect it. Check that the room offered you is not on the noisiest side overlooking route N19 and preferably not immediately next door to the W.C.

Although the local police no longer need to examine your passport when you check in at your hotel, you may occasionally be asked to leave your passport, theoretically for the gendarmerie. Madame is in fact taking precautions that you do not slip away early in the morning without paying. Just smile and remember to collect it at breakfast when you pay the bill. Incidentally, all the charges on the bill are net, i.e. 'service compris' — room, breakfast, supper, wine. There is no need to add anything more unless the service has been beyond the call of duty. If you telephone from the hotel you will be billed a premium charge. Far better to do it from the local PTT or from a Cabine de Poste. Cheap rates Monday to Friday 9.30 p.m. to 8.00 a.m., Saturdays after 2.00 p.m., Sundays and public holidays all day.

To ring the UK from France from a phonebox feed in, say, 10 francs as a credit, dial 19, wait for the tone to change, dial 44 then the STD number (less the first 0), then your number. To phone France from the UK dial 010 33, then the eight figure provincial number. You can receive calls in the box and the number is clearly marked.

Restaurants

Experienced menu-spotters, having arrived at 6.00 p.m. and parked in the main square, often select their hotel by the quality of the dinner promised for that evening. If 'rognons de veau au champagne' is on a menu and the hotel looks reasonable, that place would get my casting vote. Of course, difficulties always arise if you have say four vociferous members of the family with differing tastes. If by any chance the prix fixe menu is not handed to you by the waiter or Madame, politely but firmly ask for it. The 'plat du jour' is the chef's speciality of the day and should be well-cooked, interesting and inexpensive.

If the wine list looks too expensive and daunting, ask for a pichet or carafe of 'vin rouge/blanc/rosé du maison' which will appear rapidly at a fraction of the price of a Côte du Rhone.

Electricity

Electricity is 220 volts, so an adaptor for hairdryer or shaver is necessary with a 2 pin plug. If you are a keen reader and do not fancy French TV in the bar in the evening, take a portable lamp with a 100 watt bulb with you. The hoteliers' thrift extends from lack of soap to very low powered electric light bulbs!

Illness

If any member of your family has a relatively minor problem the pharmacie with a *green* cross will have a qualified chemist who may be able to proffer treatment and will certainly know the address of the local doctor.

Lastly, remember to drive on the right, and be prudent at crossroads, roundabouts and when coming out of a petrol station. Speed limits are clearly marked on all roads in kilometres per hour. Minor roads 90 km, dual carriageways 110 km and motorways 130 km per hour.

CHAPTER TWO:
CHAMPAGNE'S CELEBRITY
HERITAGE

A quick survey of the region shows an agricultural 'paysage' rolling away into the distance with mild slopes, occasional woods and river valleys. The famous vineyards only make up a miniscule share of the land area — some 27,000 hectares spread over two departements. The climate is almost identical to that of southern England with mild summers and often chilly winters. The Marne is the main river, which starts near Langres and is canalised northwards to St. Dizier, north west to Chalons sur Marne and westwards through Epernay and Chateau Thierry. A tributary of the Aisne passes through Reims, and further south the River Aube starts at Auberive and wanders gently northwards through Bar sur Aube before eventually joining the Seine. Troyes itself is on the River Seine. So the Champagne area is quite well watered by several rivers and the six large lakes. It is a peaceful countryside, unfortunately well-suited to military manoeuvres.

Roman arrival

Even before the Roman conquest the four local tribes were always quarrelling with each other. The Lingons around Langres, the Tricasses around Troyes, the Rèmes near Reims and the Catalaunes at Chalons sur Marne. When the Romans came in BC 58 the area was considered as belonging to the Belgians. However, Roman trade and roads soon turned Reims and Langres into important towns.

Christianity came to the Champagne area in the 2nd and 3rd century AD. Saint Sixte evangelised Reims, Saint Memmie Chalons, Saint Savinien, Troyes and Saint Bénigne —

Langres. Several centuries later Saint Loup was the bishop-soldier of Troyes and Saint Alpin at Chalons.

Attila (the flail of God) and his horrible Huns were rather surprisingly defeated in AD 451 by the Roman general Aetius. Today one can see the Camp of Attila 15 km. north east of Chalons. The Roman empire withdrew its legions and protection from the region at the end of the 5th century. Shortly afterwards Saint Remi, bishop of Reims, baptised Clovis, King of France in AD 451. This was the beginning of a tradition linking kings and their coronations to Reims. In fact, Louis the Pious was crowned there in AD 816. Twenty seven years later the treaty of Verdun divided the huge Charlemagne empire between the three sons of Louis the Pious, with the Meuse River acting as a natural barrier.

Christian revival

During the great Christian revival initiated by Saint Bernard (1090–1153) the Cistercian abbey of Clairvaux was built in AD 1115. Much of the credit goes to the Englishman Stephen Harding, Abbot of Citeaux in Burgundy, who decided to ask Bernard de Fontaine to establish a small abbey in the valley of Absinthe, later called 'la claire vallée' or Clairvaux. Sadly today the only remains of the original site, east of Bar sur Aube, are the monks' wash-house and cellars. Both Stephen Harding and Bernard de Fontaine were later canonised. At the height of their fame in AD 1153 the Cistercian order comprised 345 monasteries of which no less than 167 derived from the Champagne abbey of Clairvaux.

One interesting link with the past to be seen, concerns two of the world's most famous lovers — Abelard and Héloise. Six km. south east of Nogent sur Seine in the Aube, west north east of Troyes, is the old abbey of Paraclet. Here Abelard came to retire from the outside world about AD 1121 and his 'disciples' came from far and wide to sit at his feet (and build the abbey). Almost ten years later he moved to become an abbot in Brittany and Héloise came and took his place in AD 1129. The dead lovers now lie together in the Père Lachaise cemetery in Paris.

Years of war and wine

At the beginning of the 13th century a start was made on the building of the mighty cathedral of Reims. The trade fairs in Champagne (two at Troyes, two at Provins, one at Bar sur Aube and one at Lagny) had made the area prosperous and funds were available. Unfortunately the Hundred Years War which started in 1337 adversely affected trade and English troops were to be found frequently in Champagne country. Edward III tried to sack Reims in 1360 but luckily failed. However, in AD 1429 Joan of Arc helped crown Charles VII King in Reims Cathedral. When peace was finally declared in AD 1453 the counts and princes of Champagne were firmly absorbed into the new national monarchy.

During the 16th century the medieval arts flourished, particularly in Troyes but the so-called massacre of Wassy in March 1562 of the 'protesting' Huguenot congregation triggered off the terrible wars of religion. In fact my Huguenot ancestors arrived in London in that year, ten years before the Massacre of St. Bartholomew.

In 1654 Louis XIV was crowned at Reims and brought a long era of peace to Champagne (and the rest of France). Later in the 17th century Dom Perignon, a senior cellar monk at the abbey d'Hautvilliers (6 km. north of Epernay) discovered the phenomenon of double fermentation in bottles. Ever since, the bubbles and the fizz have largely been responsible for the prosperity of the region.

George-Jacques Danton was born at Arcis sur Aube in 1759, learned English, became a lawyer and became the effective leader of the French revolution. The *terror* caught up with him and he went to the scaffold in 1794.

Napoleonic skirmishes

A certain little Corsican corporal, Napoleon Bonaparte, studied at the military academy at Brienne le Chateau between 1779–1784. Brienne is 40 km. north east of Troyes and Boney was only aged nine when he left (for a full account see Chapter Twelve). His famous adversary, Wellington, a few years later was at the military academy of Angers on the Loire!

Napoleon's armies crossed and recrossed the Champagne plains many times but no major battles were fought there. At Valmy in September 1792 a minor battle was fought between the French under Marshal Dumouriez and the Prussians but combined casualties did not exceed 500. Two days after the battle of Valmy the new République was proclaimed.

· Early in 1814 Napoleon's armies skirmished for three months with the Allied armies under General Blucher and Schwartzenberg. A dozen minor battles were fought (Montereau, Nogent sur Seine, Mormant, Brienne le Chateau, Arcis sur Aube, Fère Champenoise, Champaubert, Vauchamps, Montmirail and Chateau Thierry). Reims and Troyes were taken and retaken by both sides.

Napoleon was fighting for his life and his reputation, as Wellington was over the Pyrenees and the odds were overwhelmingly against him. The Tsar Alexander I held a grand council at Bar sur Aube of the sorely battered Allied armies – Russians, Prussians and Austrians. Napoleon's brilliant sorties took their toll of the vast cumbersome Allied armies but it was not enough. Talleyrand and the Duke of Ragusa signed the surrender on 30th March and a week later Bonaparte abdicated at Fontainbleau.

As no British forces were employed our history books concentrate on Wellington's brilliant 'little' campaign down on the south west borders against Soult. However, the decisive battles involving three or four times the size of armies were being fought over the first three months of 1814 — on the Champagne killing grounds. When Bonaparte recaptured Reims in early 1814 — it was his last victory — his general Marmont recalled later "Reims, the last smile of Fortune". The gambler had won so often — in fact all the battles in which he commanded — except the last and final one.

The aftermath of Waterloo

After Waterloo the Allied armies of occupation numbering nearly a third of a million, were stationed around Troyes. Wellington took his lovely lady friends from Paris and Cambrai to the frequent grand reviews held in or near the Champagne towns. Marshal Drouet d'Erlon was one of Napoleon's favourites. He was born in Reims in 1765 and became general de brigade aged 24. He commanded various armies in Spain against Wellington and then at Toulouse. When the Bourbon King came back to Paris Drouet d'Erlon switched sides. He did this again, like Marshal Ney, when Bonaparte came back to brief 100 day power. After Waterloo Ney was shot and Drouet d'Erlon was condemned to death. He fled the country to run a café-brasserie in Beyrout. He was obviously a brilliant survivor — due perhaps to his liking for local champagne wines. In 1825 he returned to France, was made a Duke, became Governor-General of Algeria and was promoted to Marshal in 1843. What a man!

The Place Drouet d'Erlon in the centre of Reims is *the* place from which to start the city tour. The first of the series of Franco-Prussian wars took place in 1870. Emperor Napoleon III and his Field Marshal Mac-Mahon manoeuvered the French armies between Chalons sur Marne and Reims and finally suffered heavy defeats at Bazeilles and Sedan (just north of Champagne country). Paris was then beseiged and capitulated in January 1871. A complete victory for the Prussians.

Trench warfare

The second of the series, World War I 1914–1918, devastated the northern part of Champagne country. The first battle of the Marne was along a horseshoe front from Verdun in the east through Ruvigny, Vitry le Francois, Esternay, Coulommiers and Meaux. i.e. north of that line was occupied by Marshals Von Kluck and Von Bulow. That was the occasion when 600 Parisian taxis and some London buses sent reinforcements helter-skelter to save the line being broken.

The trench warfare front settled down for four years to a line just north of Verdun (in the east), Souain, Reims, Craonne, Soissons and Compiègne. In June 1918 the Germans made their famous breakthrough just west of Reims, 50 km. south to the edges of Chateau Thierry. The second battle of the Marne was touch and go. Marshal Foch and his 'poilus' held the line until the Armistice was signed on 11th November 1918.

Reims suffered 49 months of unrelenting bombardment from the German artillery sited a mile or so to the north. Out of 15,000 houses standing in 1914 only 3,000 survived. The city was briefly abandoned in the autumn of 1918 and many of the inhabitants took refuge in the huge subterranean chalk quarry galleries (now guarding equally vital bottled supplies!). The cathedral was hit many times but largely survived and the ravages of war were quickly repaired. Photographs of the flattened city show a swathe of destruction. Postcards are on sale in the town as a memento of the ordeal of 1914–1918.

The toast of occupation....

The third, and one hopes the final, encounter of World War II, left Champagne relatively untouched physically, although the four year occupation left its traumas. Champagne production was comparatively normal and the occupying forces drank it with gusto.

...and liberation

So, must I add, did the British liberating armies in 1944–1945. Certainly, the 11th Armoured Division, in which I served, acquired enormous supplies more or less legitimately from the defeated and fleeing Wehrmacht. I was aged twenty then, enjoyed the bubble and fizz enormously and have done so ever since. On 7th May 1945 the Armistice was signed in Reims which was an appropriate place.

De Gaulle's resting place

The most recent Champagne celebrity was General Charles de Gaulle, who in 1933 purchased a handsome property at Colombey les Deux Eglises in the lee of the hill. He retired there initially in 1946 and again in 1969.

He died there on 9th November 1970 and a vast cross of Lorraine can be seen from many miles away, on top of the 400 metre hill. He is buried in the small village cemetery which is now almost a pilgrimage site.

CHAPTER THREE: GRAND TOUR

If you can spare a fortnight then I recommend the following grand tour.

- Reims (two days)
- Chalons (one day)
- Chaumont (one day)
- Langres (one day)
- Troyes (two days)
- Provins (one day)
- Epernay (one day)

I'm sure you will find this tour a delightful way to spend two weeks. To give you some indication of the treats in store I have included in this chapter a brief description of each of the proposed stops.

Reims (pop. 185,000)

Although Chalons sur Marne is the préfecture town of the Champagne area, Reims is the largest city, both in terms of culture (2,000 years old) and wine it has more to offer. So I have chosen it as the most appropriate starting and ending point for my grand tour. It is easily reached from Paris by the autoroute No. 4 (140 km.), from Brussels (213 km.), from Luxembourg to the east (232 km.) or from Dijon to the south east (283 km.). The A4 follows the canal de la Marne and the River Vesle through the southern part of the city.

The airport of Reims-Champagne is due north of the town, 3 km. on the D74 at Betheny. There are flights to 11 destinations including Madrid and Rome, but not direct to the UK. Tel: 26 07 18 85. The rail journey to the Gare de l'Est in

The cathedral at Reims

Paris takes 1½ hours to cover the 154 km.

Reims has the superb Cathedral of Nôtre Dame (see Chapters Eight and Nine) with the famous Smiling Angel on the facade, stained glass windows by Chagall, its tapestries and treasury next door in the Palace of Tau. The Basilique and Museum of St. Remi is 800 metres south east in a quiet square.

The main shopping centre is to the north and west of the Cathedral together with many enticing restaurants and speciality shops. The main market is in the rue de Mars and the railway station 400 metres south west down the Boulevard Foch. Parking is not particularly easy but try along the length of the public gardens which stretch for 1 km. between the station and the main town.

A dozen or more Champagne houses offer tasting facilities (see Chapter Five) many within walking distance eastwards from the Basilique. There are half a dozen excellent museums including St. Denis, Vieux Reims and St. Remi. A major pilgrimage of St. Remi takes place the first week of October and the Fête of Joan of Arc is on the 8th May.

The town has several good value budget hotels. Try the Hotel d'Alsace, 6 rue General Sarrail (26 47 44 08), nice owner, near the station and the market. The Place Drouet d'Erlon has many brasseries and small restaurants. Try the Restaurant Colbert or the aux Coteaux Champenois.

Reims is definitely worth a two day stay — more if you wish to try out the various regional tours including Epernay to the south.

At the start of the grand tour take the N44 due east towards Chalons sur Marne which is 45 km. away. The road runs parallel to the River Vesle and the autoroute 4. The Fort de la Pompelle is 9 km. out of Reims. The massive fort was constructed in 1880 to protect the outskirts of the city. The Germans took it for three weeks in September 1914 but it was retaken and helped win the two battles of the Marne. Its height of 120 metres makes it a good vantage point. There are several delightful wine villages a few kilometres south including Sillery, Verzy and Beaumont sur Vesle.

Chalons sur Marne (pop. 55,000)

Chalons sur Marne is the administrative centre of the Champagne-Ardenne area. The 13th century Cathedral of St. Etienne has beautiful stained glass windows and treasury. Irish readers will be interested to see the mitre and a shoe which belonged to St. Malachie, an early Irish missionary.

The Church of Notre Dame en Vaux is 400 metres east of the cathedral overlooking a canal or tributary of the River Marne, which skirts the western side of the town. The cloisters and museum of Notre Dame en Vaux are worth a visit.

Chalons does not have the grandeur of Reims but it has a serenity of its own, brought about by the gracious river, parks, canal, dignified old 'hôtels' (town mansions), three museums and magnificent churches. There is even a Jardin Anglais overlooking the river and boat tours. Champagne Joseph Perrier accepts visits.

The SNCF station (Paris two hours) is 500 metres west of the town centre, a quarter of an hour's walk away. There are half a dozen small hotels — try La Comédie, the Chemin de Fer or the Au Bon Accueil. Good champenois meals can be had at the restaurants Les Années Folles, L'Etape, Le Poélon and several others including Le Sulky. The Syndicat d'Initiative run an excellent city tour lasting two to three hours for 12 francs, July — September excluding Sundays and Mondays. There are several regional tours possible from Chalons.

Vitry le Francois (pop. 19,000)

From Chalons keep south east for 32 km. on the same N44 towards Vitry le Francois. The road runs on the eastern side of the River Marne. The town has an unfortunate history. Known originally as Vitry en Perthois it was destroyed in 1544 by the army of King Charles V. It was beautifully rebuilt and renamed, only to be destroyed by the Germans in the spring and summer of 1940. Again rebuilt in the postwar period, it has a surviving 17th century church, Hotel de Ville and a Louis XIV town gate.

In Vitry the hotel/restaurant Au Bon Sejour is appropriately good value! Keep heading south east on the N4 towards St. Dizier, 20 km. away via Villiers en Lieu.

St. Dizier (pop. 40,000)

This was once a Roman spa town and is now mainly industrial. It has had an interesting historical background. The original pre-Roman tribe was called 'Les Bragards' and they put up strong resistance to King Charles V in 1544, who called the inhabitants 'les braves gars'. Napoleon won his final victory here when he harried the Russians out of the town in January and again in March 1814.

The Hotel Picardy and the Restaurant L'Est are good value. Two canals bisect the town and the hotel de ville has the original 1228 town Charter. A local excursion north east on the N401 to Bar le Duc and to the abbey of Trois Fontaines is recommended. To the south west is the large Lac du Der Chantecoq and the village of Montier en Der. The word Der is celtic for Chêne, since the oak forests are a feature of the countryside.

Joinville (pop. 5,000)

From St. Dizier, either via Bar le Duc, or south east 31 km. to Joinville again destroyed by the horrible King Charles V in 1544. The inhabitants 'Les Joinvillois' then promptly built the Chateau du Grand Jardin which is definitely worthwhile looking at. The Hotel du Nord, the Poste and Soleil d'Or are good value hotel/restaurants.

Chaumont (pop. 29,000)

Then due south on the D67 via Vignory which has an 11th century church of St. Etienne with clocktower — one of the best in Champagne — to Chaumont where the old Counts of Champagne lived in the 13th century. The 12th century castle keep is a feature as is the 19th century viaduct over the River Suize (in three stages 300 metres long and 52 metres high). In 1814 the treaty of Chaumont was signed by the Allies, Austria,

Russia, Prussia and England, who jointly decided to continue the war until Napoleon was defeated. The town was later occupied by the Prussians in 1871. German bombardments in 1940 and 1944 badly damaged the town. The 13th century Basilique Church of St. John the Baptist, the castle keep and several other historical sites make Chaumont worth a detailed visit.

The hotel/restaurants of Le Grand Val and Etoile d'Or are both good value. Chaumont is the prefecture town of the Haute Marne. It is a small, heavily wooded departement and several forest tours are organised by the Office du Tourisme opposite the railway station. In addition to the 250,000 hectares of forests there are 2,300 km. of rivers and canals mostly navigable by canoe/kayak. Bicycles can also be rented to tour one or more of the ten circuits around Chaumont. The Faubourg des Tanneries overlooks the town — for centuries the skin tanners of Chaumont were well known.

Langres (pop. 11,200)

The N19 due south to Langres for 35 km. runs parallel and to the west of the river/canal of the Marne. To the east are the towns of Bourmont, Nogent en Bassigny and the spa town of Bourbonne les Bains. These are best visited either from Chaumont or Langres. Immediately to the east of Langres are two large lakes (Charmes and la Lieze) and to the west two more (La Manche and Villequsien). For centuries Langres was a walled, fortified town which was one of the three capitals of Gallic Burgundy. It is one of the 'portes de Bourgogne'. Indeed Dijon is only 68 km. to the south on the A31 or N74.

Langres was an archbishopric for hundreds of years and the Cathedral St. Mamme's was originally built in the 12th century. The town is built on a small hill and the 2½ miles of ramparts encircle the town, from which one has a superb view of the valley of the Marne. There are seven towers and six town gates, one of which is Roman. Langres was the capital of the Lingons, an important Gallic tribe. There are several medieval streets to walk through in the centre. Unexpectedly the long established trade is that of cutlery making. However, for 400 years the town has had a reputation for culture. The Association Orchésographie 88 mounts ballet, concerts, theatre, debates, street-fêtes and 'spectacles'. Try the Auberge Jeanne d'Arc or les Moulins — both have restaurants.

The next step on the grand tour is Colombey les Deux Eglises — General de Gaulle's home. Take the N19 north and after a few km. turn left and west to Arc en Barrois for 30 km. and then north on the D65, D6 and D23 to Colombey. It is a small sleepy village but is the resting place of France's greatest soldier and politician of this century. He may have said 'Non' to us too frequently; he may have abused our wartime help and hospitality; but he was a great leader of the French — 'La France, c'est moi'. As a result hundreds of travellers of all nationalities come to pay their respects to this great man. He gave France hope, dignity and self-respect for several decades.

Bar sur Aube (pop. 4,000)

This town is 15 km. west of Colombey on the N19 and not to be confused with Bar sur Seine 37 km. to the south west or Bar le Duc north east of St. Dizier. The Counts of Bar were once a power in the land and built chateaux to protect their widespread towns. Poor forgotten Clairvaux is a few kilometres south east of Bar sur Aube.

Bar sur Aube is in the departement of the Aube and is the centre of the southern champagne area which is a rectangle heading south west to Bar sur Seine. The two 'vignobles' are known as Bar sur Aubois and Bar Séquanais (see Chapter Six) and 60 small villages (covering 4,000 hectares) are deeply involved in the champagne-making process. This is a cheerful bustling little town and would make an ideal centre for an unsophisticated wine tour of the region. You might as well be several thousand miles away from Reims and Epernay — but the quality is good, nearly as good as the big names. Try staying at the hotel/restaurant le Commerce (XXX) or the Pomme d'Or.

The next stop is Troyes, 52 km. due west through the Forest d'Orient. Between la Villeneuve en Chene and Lusigny sur Barse and to the north side of the road is the huge man-made

Hotel in Aube – Troyes

lake d'Orient of 2,300 hectares (6,000 acres) which has an animal park, an ornithological reserve and sailing, swimming and fishing facilities (see Chapter Twenty).

Troyes (pop. 65,000)

The N19 continues westwards into Troyes, the préfecture town of the Aube. Apart from a disastrous fire in 1524 the centre of Troyes has suffered little from the ravages of time. Its famous bishop St. Loup persuaded Attila the Hun not to sack the town — a miracle if ever there was one! The three wars with Germany left few scars and so the centre is still a medieval gem! Narrow streets with tall dignified half-timbered gabled houses give the town much character.

The River Seine encircles the north and north east sectors and there are wooded parks along the Boulevard Gambetta and Boulevard Carnot on the west and south sides, making the old town shaped like a champagne cork. Not that this is champagne country. Troyes was famous in the Middle Ages for the great trade fairs which brought merchants in from all over Europe, celebrated now in June. As a result two disparate local industries grew up and prospered. The most important 'pays des bonnets de coton' now has 300 firms with nearly 20,000 people employed in making hosiery products. This is still big business in France if less so in the UK. The second local business is 'les Andouillettes de Troyes' — sausages, bacon and pig derivatives of all shapes and colour.

My wife and I stayed at the old fashioned Hotel Le Marigny in the medieval town and had an excellent (economic) meal in the rue de General Saussier, near the Place du Marché au Pain. In the ruelle des Chats the felines are now quite scarce. One of the early Counts of Champagne, Henry I, founded 13 churches and 13 hospitals in Troyes. Besides the Cathedral of St. Pierre and St. Paul and the Basilique St. Urbain, there are six others worth a visit. Troyes also has half a dozen excellent museums although curiously enough the best known is the Museum of Modern Art founded as recently as 1976. The Derain oil paintings of London sights should be seen, as well as those by Braque, Vlaminck and van Dongen. The museum

29

is next to the cathedral.

Our history books record the Treaty of Troyes signed in May 1420 by Charles VI and Queen Isabel of Bavaria with the English as an act of diplomacy. The French call it shameful and treasonable especially since our jolly soldier-king Henry V married Catherine of France (Queen Isabel's daughter) in the Troyes church of St. Jean. It is worth a visit for that reason alone! The cathedral has famous stained glass windows and a rich Byzantine treasury. St. Panthaleon is in effect a museum church. The Renaissance mansions or 'hôtels' to see are Vauluisant, Autruy, Chapelaine, Marisy, Ursins and Mauroy.

If I had the opportunity of spending a week in just one place in the Champagne area, Troyes would have my vote every time, ahead of Reims. There are many budget hotels here. Try the Hotel du Theatre or La Mascotte, both with restaurants. There are many excursions possible from Troyes mainly in the south, the 'Pays d'Othe' including Isle Aumont, Rumilly les Vaudes, Chaource and Ervy le Chatel.

The N19 continues north west from Troyes running west and parallel to the River Seine, via Fontaine les Gres, Pont sur Seine (see the chateau) to Nogent sur Seine.

Nogent sur Seine (pop. 5,000)

This pleasant town with its many half timbered houses is almost an island encircled by the Seine. A quick tour will establish connections with Henri IV, Napoleon, Gustave Flaubert, Paul Claudel and many others. Louis XIV so admired the 15th century Church of St. Laurent with its 130 foot tower that he called the city 'Nogent with the beautiful tower'.

The museum is well known and the chateau of Motte Tilly (perhaps the finest in Champagne) is 6 km. south west overlooking the river (April — December visits). Do not forget to ask for the abbey of Paraclet founded by Abelard for his Héloise, 6 km. south east on the N19 and D442. Try the hotel/restaurant le Beau Rivage on the banks of the Seine.

Provins (pop. 13,000)

Technically Provins on the D74, 18 km. to the west, is just outside Champagne but it is so close, so pretty and interesting that it is worth such a modest detour. In the Middle Ages Troyes and Provins, both with two Grand Fairs each year dominated the commercial sector in north east France. In the 13th century Provins' population was over 60,000 — a very respectable size in those days. The old medieval town surrounded by ramparts is on a hill to the west side. The Tourist Office is sited by the famous Julius Caesar's Tower.

The English link with Provins is provided by Edmund of Lancaster's marriage with the widow of Henri le Gros, Comte de Champagne in the 13th century. He thus became the ruler from afar of Provins! The red rose of Lancaster (versus the white rose of York) derived from the red roses grown in Provins. Thibaut IV, Comte de Provence, brought the rose plants back from Jericho during the Fourth Crusade. Edmund incorporated the red rose of Provins (or Jericho) in his coat of arms. The rose growers of Provins are still well known (Roserie J. Vizier). Several rivers bisect and trisect Provins, making it a most intriguing town to visit. Try the hotel/restaurant la Croix d'Or or la Fontaine.

Sezanne (pop. 6,200)

The D403 north east via Villiers St. Georges leads one back towards Champagne country. The chateau d'Esternay is on the left of the river and the forest of la Traconne on the right before one comes into Sezanne which is back in the Marne departement. Try the local still white wine at the hotel/restaurant Croix d'Or.

The N51 leads towards Epernay which is 44 km. due north. Soon one passes through the Marais de St. Goud, a large swampy plain covering 3,000 hectares (7,500 acres), where the first battle of the Marne took place between the German 2nd Army under Von Bulow and General Foch's 9th French Army. Next is Mont Aimé, a small hill of 240 metres, which dominates the plain. From prehistoric times it was fortified and made into a feudal chateau but alas now is ruined. The Duke of Wellington attended the huge Russian Army review here on 10th September 1815. To the right of the road is the chateau d'Etoges. The elegant 17th century red brick chateau is in good repair and worth a visit.

Montmort Lucy is another elegant chateau. Built in the 16th century it was acquired by Sully and can be seen from the N51.

Epernay (pop. 28,876)

19 km. ahead is this unashamedly rich, well laid out town dominated by the Champagne barons. Although a sixth of the size of Reims it competes strongly as **the** champagne town. The elegant Avenue de la Champagne is the D3 east of the central Place Republique. The largest champagne house of all is Moet et Chandon, and the Mercier group is now second in volume. Champagne de Castellane is based in the same notable road and all three offer sophisticated tours. Moet et Chandon have *28 km.* of caves, Mercier 18 km. and de Castellane a modest 10 km. — just think of the scale! As Moet has 75 million bottles of bubbly in stock, there must be tens of millions of pounds of investment locked up 'sub terra'.

The Museum of Champagne and Archaeology in the same Avenue de Champagne makes for an interesting visit. Epernay makes an excellent centre for a wine tour of the regions (see Chapter Five). Epernay is so prosperous that hotels and restaurants tend to be out of the budget range. The Hotel la Terrasse overlooking the River Marne is excellent value. Try their Foie gras de Canard and Matelotte de Rivière au Vin d'Ay.

Epernay is the end of my grand tour. Across the river Marne, the N51 is only 27 km. from Reims where we started. The Montagne de Reims is very steep indeed, surrounded by wine villages and is part of the Parc naturel region de la Montagne de Reims. Curious trees, twisted trunks in fantastic shapes called 'Les Faix de Verzy' are one of the sights (see Chapter Twenty).

UK Tour companies

Code: AHA=art, history & architecture, BH=birdwatching holidays, BT=battlefield tours, C=camping, CH=chateaux, CT= coach tours, G=gîte, H=hotels, M=motorway, SB=short breaks, SC=senior citizens, WT=wine tours

Arblaster & Clarke	7 Hilltops Court, 65 North Lane, Buriton, PETERSFIELD GU31 5RS. Tel. 0730 66883	G-V SB-WT
Argosy Holidays	P.O. Box 100, HALESOWEN, W.Midlands B63 3BT. Tel. 021 550 7401	M
Aries Holidays	56 Joyce Road, BUNGAY, Suffolk NR35 1LA. Tel. 0986 5552	H
Blackheath Wine Trails	13 Blackheath Village, LONDON SE3 9LD. Tel.01 463 0012	WT
Branta Travel	11 Uxbridge Street, LONDON W8 7TQ. Tel. 01 229 7231	BH
Canterbury Travel	248 Streatfield Road, Kenton, HARROW, Middx. Tel. 01 206 0411	H
Canvas Holidays	Bull Plain, HERTFORD, Herts. SG14 1DY. Tel. 0992 553535	C-H-SB SC
Cosmos	Cosmos House, 1 Bromley Common, BROMLEY, Kent. Tel. 01 464 3121	H-SB
Country Special Holidays	153B Kidderminster Road, BEWDLEY DY12 1JE. Tel. 0299 403528	WT
Eurobreaks	Sunsites House, DORKING, Surrey RH4 1YZ. Tel. 0306 886122	SB-H
French Leave	21 Fleet Street, LONDON EC4. Tel. 01 583 8383	SB-H
French Selection	407 London House, 26–40 Kensington High Street, LONDON W8 4PF. Tel. 01 938 4588	H-Ch
Global Continental	Intasun House, Cromwell Avenue, BROMLEY, Kent. Tel. 01 464 9696	CT
Hamptonhouse Travel	49 Fife Road, KINGSTON UPON THAMES, Surrey KT1 1BG. Tel. 01 549 2116	SB-H
JAC Travel	15 Albert Mews, LONDON W8 5RU. Tel. 01 581 5055	SB-H

CHAMPAGNE ON A BUDGET

Just France	Eternit House, Felsham Road, LONDON SW15 1SF. Tel. 01 788 3878	SB-H
Major Holts Battlefield Tours	Golden Key Building, 15 Market Street, SANDWICH, Kent. Tel. 0304 612248	BT
David Newman	P.O. Box 733, Upperton Road, EASTBOURNE, Sussex BN21 4AW. Tel. 0323 410347	SB-H
P&O European Ferries	Enterprise House, Channel View Road, DOVER, Kent. Tel. 0304 203388	SB-H
Slipaway Holidays	90 Newlands Road, WORTHING, West Sussex. Tel. 0903 821000	SB-CT
Swan Hellenic Tours	77 New Oxford Street, LONDON WC1A 1PP. Tel. 01 831 1616	AHA
Travel Associates	17 Nottingham Street, LONDON W1M 3RD. Tel. 01 935 7618	SB-WT
Travellers	37 Bridge House, Shepherds Lane, LONDON E9 6JL. Tel. 01 533 2486	SB-WT
Vacances en Campagne	Bignor, nr. PULBOROUGH, W. Sussex. Tel. 07987 366	G-V-SB
David Walker Travel	10B Littlegate Street, OXFORD OX1 1QT. Tel. 0865 728136	WT
Wessex Continental Travel	124 North Road East, PLYMOUTH, Devon. Tel. 0752 228333	SB-H
World Wine Tours	4 Dorchester Rd, DRAYTON St. LEONARD, Oxon. OX9 8BH. Tel. 0865 891919	WT

Holidays afloat

The following UK based companies offer canal or barge holidays in the Champagne area.

Blakes Holidays	WROXHAM, Norwich, Norfolk NR12 8DH. Tel. 0603 3224
Enterprise Charter Cruises	2A Southmoor, BUCKLEIGH, Bideford, Devon. Tel. 02372 75024
French Country Cruises	19 Churchill Way, Painswick, STROUD, Glos. Tel. 0452 812685
Renaissance	91 Piedwick Lane, Sandal, WAKEFIELD, W. Yorks. Tel. 0924 258143

CHAPTER FOUR:
BUBBLES AND FIZZ

Why does the world, and particularly the British, drink so much champagne? After the French, the British market is the largest in the world, more than the vast USA, more than the affluent Germans (who do have their own Sekt sparkling wine). Doctor Sigmund Freud would have had a field day studying and analysing why the Anglo Saxon tribes in our offshore island drink so much champagne. He would have started with the various cosy nicknames for the drink. "Champers" is used perhaps more frequently by the landed gentry, the city and the professional race-goers. Fizz, a spot of Fizz and Bucks Fizz emanate from London's masculine clubland — Whites, Boodles and the rest. Bubbly to me means late Edwardian Gaiety Girls and their dashing admirers who, rumour has it, drank champagne out of their dancing shoes — well chacun à son gout! 'Come and have a glass of champagne' echoes round the country day after day, night after night.

Celebration ritual

It is someone's birthday, their anniversary, their wedding day. Mr. A. is celebrating a new job. Mr. B. has lost his job and drowning his sorrows in Bubbly! Mrs. C. has a new baby so out comes the Champers! Mr. D. is retiring and we must speed him on his way. Miss E. has got herself engaged! When this book is finished and launched the author and his wife will celebrate with some Fizz — and so it goes on! Derby Day, or Ascot or the Grand National or the Boat Race, or we have won/lost the Ashes — there are no excuses, only good reasons for cracking a bottle.

First, however, the ritual. The host with strong hands and a sense of direction, produces the bottle (probably just out of the fridge) and checks it is cold enough, and contemplates showing the label (either discreetly, proudly or blatantly) to his assembled guests. Although Messrs. J. Sainsbury sell more bottles in the UK of their excellent champagne (at an excellent) price) than even Moet et Chandon, the betting is that their label is rarely displayed. Snobbism dies hard in our country. Krug or 'The Widow' is another matter altogether!

Then comes the fumbling to get the foil off the top of the bottle, and to unfasten the wire cage *without* shaking it. Tricky business this, particularly if it is the third or fourth bottle. Now the desperate battle begins to get the stubborn cork out. Often it defies its owner for many minutes (I know the feeling of *despair* when nothing gives at all, and the delicate ladies are getting thirstier all the time). The permutations of success or failure are many. Total disaster is either when the cork erupts unannounced with great velocity and damages (a) the host (b) his wife or (c) a guest. Failing that the dog or the chandeliers are suitable targets. Still worse is to come — a quarter of the bottle is on the carpet and the glasses are a few feet away! It takes a strong steady hand, lots of practice over the years and a certain amount of luck. So, Sigmund would have studied the cosy nomenclature and the elaborate fumbling ritual to conquer the foaming beast.

Now comes the *noise*! A huge explosion of sound means psychological (social) success and encouraging mutters from all around. Conversely, a soft low-key little 'phutt' means social disaster — the 'Champers' simply cannot be good if the sound does not echo round the house to 'aahs' and 'ohs'. All the host can do is to pour out the bottle quickly, shaking it unobtrusively to coax a little more life into the failing bubbles. Sigmund would have a marvellous time studying this scene. Does Man master the Bottle or the reverse? What of the Social Stigma or Success?

Any time, any place

Some people drink champagne at noon (surely not before then?). Perhaps King Edward VII (before he became King and was the Doyen of Cannes with assorted decorative mistresses) drank champers for breakfast. Come to think of it, he *must* have done, if the all-night gambling at the casino or baccarat with his mates at private parties, continued to and past dawn. The Folies Bergeres girls with their damp slippers helped him celebrate — but what? Being alive, I suppose, having lots of money, time and the inclination. George Laybourne sang 'Champagne Charlie is my name' on the Victorian boards in 1869 and helped the wine's popularity. My grandfather who was in the wine trade (like most of my family) produced champers at the drop of a hat. It was always drunk as an aperitif. The French and our own British wine shippers drink it during the meal to accompany fish, meat, even cheese.

R.S. Surtees put these words into his jolly Mr. Jorrocks' mouth in Paris 'Champagne certainly gives one werry gentlemanly ideas, but for a continuance, I don't know but I should prefer mild (h)ale'. Lady Mary Wortley Montague, the indefatigable traveller of the 18th century wrote in her book "The Lover" 'And we meet, with champagne and a chicken, at last' — which to me is a most romantic turn of phrase.

So we have gentlemanly feelings and romance for our Austrian Doctor to consider, but what of the colour? According to the grapes used the wine colour ranges from a deep dark gold to a pale delicate straw-coloured wine often with greeny streaks. Pink champagne is making a strong comeback. Once it was definitely a cad's wine linked intimately with the Gaiety Girls and the dancing, song-birds of London and Paris. It is not everyone's taste but it has a saucy nonchalance to it.

Matter of taste

Vintage champagnes (and 1982, 1983 and 1985 were good single-year vintages) are considerably more expensive but sell well to the well-heeled cognoscenti — the same people who have the knowledge and experience and opportunity to drink selected champagnes during and after their meals. Vintage champagnes now account for 15% of the big shippers' sales.

The tradition in the UK is that we prefer our wines dry, rather than sweet and this applies to champagne, but there are

Wines in store

variations on a theme of dryness. *Extra Brut* is really very dry indeed (i.e. with only 0–6 grammes of sugar content per litre), *Brut* has less than 15 grammes per litre, *Extra Dry* has 12–20 grammes per litre and then we come to *Sec* which has 17–35 grammes. The two final categories rarely to be seen in the UK are *Demi-Sec* at 33–50 grammes per litre and *Doux* at more than 50 grammes per litre. So when one buys a bottle of *Dry* champagne, i.e. *Sec* there are no less than three drier categories! Incidentally, my years in the wine trade taught me that although one or more of these classifications may be currently more popular than the rest, it has no relation to the wine's intrinsic quality. One drinks, or should drink, only what one *really* likes and palates, thank goodness, are different!

A few final words before the rather more technical chapters.

Glasses

These vary enormously in style and size. Some are round, saucer-shaped and flat, some are flute or tulip-shaped. My grandfather preferred the former and I prefer the latter. He said he could *see* what he was drinking. I say that I am protecting the costly bubbles and can see the colour better. Who is right? Anyway, if someone gives you a Yuppy Swizzle Stick as a present, hand it back to them quickly. It is a silly affectation to reduce the bubble content so lovingly created.

Bottles

A standard 75 centilitre bottle accounts for over 90% of sales, but once opened please do finish it. A flat champagne drunk the following day is a sad reminder of its previous glory. Half bottles are more expensive to buy but are ideal for couples as an aperitif — just the right amount. A full bottle allows for six generous glasses and a half bottle for three reasonable glasses. Much larger bottles are available for parties. Magnum (2), Jereboam (4), Rehoboam (6), Methusaleh (8), Salmanazar (12) and believe it or not, Balthazar (16) and Nebuchadnezzar (20) bottles.

Temperature

Please do not drink your bubbly *too* cold, or for that matter *too* warm. One hour in the fridge should produce a perfect 45°F (75°C).

Gastronomic considerations

The Sunday Times published an article in May 1987 about 'A Champagne Diet' launched by Debrett's Peerage publications written by Joan Oliphant-Fraser, a former ballerina and author of the diet. Basically it recommends the consumption of four bottles of vintage champagne per week. Apparently champagne contains certain minerals, acids and enzymes which help the metabolism of fat and aid the digestive system. The author goes on to say that bubbly can 'change your outlook on life by promoting a champagne personality — effervescent, positive and larger than life!' She says 'Champagne also acts as a diuretic, but I didn't like to mention that because it's dreary and medical!' The health farm Champneys said that 'Half a bottle of champagne a day is really too much. We recommend a maximum of two bottles a week and no more than one glass a day on a calorie controlled diet' — the meanies! The Royal College of Psychiatrists were even more depressing — but then that's their job in life. Debrett's final word was 'Four glasses a day is perfectly permissable but nobody can seriously think they will lose weight if they get blind drunk *every* day.' I like the use of the word '*every*'. Of course the French rather grandiloquently call champagne 'The Wine of Kings and the King of Wines'. I am sure Debrett's would agree.

Storage

One final word of advice. If you store a case or two, or a number of bottles in the house (a) keep them lying flat so that the cork is in touch with the wine, (b) out of sunlight and (c) in a stable, preferably cool spot. Wines hate variable temperature. (d) Do not for instance *keep* a bottle permanently in the fridge and never in the freezer. Make sure your friends give you one hour's notice before they arrive. Remind your lady guests that

Madame de Pompadour in the 18th century declared that 'Champagne was the only wine that leaves a woman beautiful after drinking it'.

Drama in ten acts

Champagne parties are usually great fun *but* there can be moments of great drama — for instance:

1.   The host wrestles in public and unsuccessfully to release the cork (incidentally never twist it, always prise gently but firmly). It will not come out. Strong male guests fidget because if they proffer help it implies their host is pretty useless at this particular job and weedy to boot! Meanwhile the host is in despair — what to do?

2.   The cork comes out eventually and hits the host's eye, causing early retirement. What does the hostess do?

3.   The cork comes out and not only hits the guest of honour painfully but the froth ruins his or her dress or suit. What does the host do? If she is his mother-in-law, rumour soon spreads that the host meant to do it.

4.   Alternatively the guest of honour is young, pretty and her soaked dress needs urgent attention. The host is first to offer help.

5.   The host's dog takes fright at the cork's ejection noise, becomes hysterical, runs amok and bites some (or all) of the guests.

6.   The bottle spills so much of the contents on the carpet and (4) above that all the guests feel guilty and spend the next half hour mopping up.

7.   The host serves *tepid* champagne to a guest in the wine trade.

8.   The host serves *flat* champagne to everyone. That awful feeling when no noise is heard as the cork quietly slides out.

9.   The host has served ice-cold champagne, everyone's taste buds are frozen and the wine tastes of very cold nothing.

10.   The champagne party is so noisy that uninvited guests *and* the police turn up at the same time. Oh well!

CHAPTER FIVE:
CHAMPAGNE PRODUCTION

Vines were growing in the Champagne area *before* the Romans came. Fossil vine leaves of the tertiary age prove this beyond doubt but the Roman legionnaires drank Italian, Spanish or Provencal wine! The fairs in the Middle Ages of Troyes and Provins allowed many foreign traders to sample and buy the local wine. However, it never was and is not even now, a particularly exciting *still* wine! Even so, Cardinal Wolsey was sent the 'vin d'Ay' in 1518. The English taverners imported the wine of Sillery (south east of Reims) in the 17th century and often found the secondary fermentation caused bubbles and effervescence (Charles II drank sparkling 'vin gris' in 1660).

Dom Perignon's breakthrough

Dom Perignon (1639–1715) the cellarer and steward of the Abbey of Hautvilliers, at the end of the 17th century succeeded in mastering this fermentation and obtained a *clear* wine with constant effervescence. His statue stands proudly in the great courtyard outside Moet et Chandon in Epernay. "Brothers, brothers" he cried out at the time, "come quickly, I am drinking stars". Remember, those were the days when glass bottles were unreliable in strength, corks as we know them today totally unheard of, and primitive methods were used of keeping the stopper from exploding outwards.

Afterwards Voltaire wrote 'Of this fresh wine, the sparkling froth is the brilliant image of our French people". From 1820 shipments of champagne achieved great popularity and began to leave the cellars of Reims, Epernay and Ay by the millions.

Napoleon before Waterloo said "In victory you deserve it, in defeat you need it".

The terrible Phylloxera parasite disease decimated the Champagne vineyards in 1890–1910. The grafted vines on safe American stock meant an expensive, major replanting operation. The area is strictly defined and controlled. The total of 60,000 acres has been planted, although this is slowly increasing, by 500 hectares each year, until the legal total of 84,000 acres (33,000 hectares) is reached. The departement of the Marne accounts for 21,000 hectares (77.8%), the Aube for 4,600 (17%) and the Aisne departement (around Chateau Thierry) for 1,400 (5.2%). A total of 250 villages are authorised to produce champagne of which 180 are in the Marne, nearly 70 in the Aube and 5 in the Aisne.

Production figures

Annual production figures vary enormously depending on a variety of problems set by nature. Too hot, too cold, too much rain, too little rain, hailstorms in the spring, can wreck the vintage potential as can mildew, etc. For instance, the vintage in 1978 and 1981 yielded 79 and 92 million bottles and 1982, 1983, 1986 and 1987 between 260 and 302 million bottles! The relatively cold climate (equivalent to Sussex) produces slightly acidic non-ripe grapes ideal for the final dry blended wine; brisk acidity in fact.

Grape varieties

The three grape varieties that match the Champagne thick chalky sub-soil are Pinot Noir (36%) and Pinot Meunier (36%) (both are black skinned grapes which yield white juice) and the white Chardonnay grape (28%). The chalky soil is ideal for these vines. It stores the heat of the sun and reflects warmth to the roots. Drainage is perfect and yet enough humidity is retained in the soil to nourish the roots. The chalk has mineral elements to give the champagne grapes certain characteristics.

The yield per hectare (2½ acres) is legally limited to 1 hectolitre for 150 kilograms weight of grapes (26.4 gallons per

43

330 lbs. weight of grapes). Note that 1.66 kilograms of grapes produce one bottle. The first grape pressing is called the 'cuvée' and the next two pressings the 'première taille' and 'deuxième taille'. Only the juice from these three pressings may be used to make champagne. The vin de Cuvée naturally has the best, freshest quality and accounts for 10/13ths (or 10 out of 13 casks); the première taille 2/13ths (or 2 casks) and finally the deuxième taille 1/13th (1 cask).

Getting technical

At harvest time (100 days after the spring flowering) usually in October, the grape picking is done by hand. In most areas of France huge machine-tractors ('enjambeurs') which straddle the vines and beat or thrash the grape bunches off are being introduced. Only the best grapes are selected for the champagne appellation and the average vine lives for 30–35 years. The Pinot Meunier grape has greater finesse, less 'gout de terroir' than the Pinot Noir.

The grape juice ('must') is put into 205 litre oak casks or large open vats for the first fermentation, i.e. the natural sugar content changes chemically into alcohol, so 11% of sugar content will produce, if totally fermented, 11% of alcohol. After the first fermentation the grape juice now becomes a cloudy young wine, but over the winter the still wine becomes clear or clearer as the wine lees separate and fall to the bottom. At that stage the young wine from each separate vineyard is carefully assessed.

Now 85% of champagnes are blends of many individual vineyards. Each champagne shipper skilfully maintains his standard blend of 30–40 selected vineyards by constant tasting. The permutations are considerable since grape varieties, different vineyards and the differing annual vintage results all pose new factors. When blending of the young wine is completed a small quantity of cane sugar and yeast is added to produce a second fermentation in the bottle, which is now corked and stacked on its side 'sur lattes' in the dark cool champagne cellars. This is the first stage (Tirage) successfully completed.

The added yeast and sugar cause the second fermentation within the stoppered bottles, producing fine bubbles and a light and persistent froth called 'mousse'. Now the wine must stay for a minimum of 12 months (three years for vintage unblended wines), but with the bigger, well-funded champagne houses, usually up to three years for all their wines. The bottles are kept on a sloping rack, head down. When the time comes for the final stage, the bottles are turned a quarter turn *each day by hand* to allow the deposit (dead yeast cells) formed in the bottle to slide down the bottle onto the cork. The skilled 'rémueurs' turn 30,000 bottles per day.

The next skilled operation is called the 'degorgement' when the bottle neck is frozen and the cork is extracted with its deposit and an equal volume of champagne plus cane sugar (no yeast), the 'dosage' is added to produce one of the permutations required from *Extra Brut* through to *Doux*. The filled bottle then receives the final cork (branded appropriately) and a label to authenticate its provenance.

- The Chef de Caves is responsible for making up the Cuvées, sometimes in oak fermentation vats or into oak 'foudres', but now alas more realistically into glass-lined steel containers. He is the manager of 'Le Chantier' — the skilled team.

- The 'Remuer' twists, turns and shakes two handedly, up to 20,000 or even 30,000 bottles a day on their sloping pupitres. Alas he too is gradually being replaced by riddling machines called gyropalettes. These are square cages holding about 40 dozen bottles which are set electronically to reproduce the riddling movements that man has done so well since Dom Perignon saw stars.

- The 'Dégorgeur' is another skilled member of the team who supervises the freezing of the neck of every full bottle prior to disgorging the small ice-block of frozen wine deposit and then replacing it with more wine.

- Monsieur le 'Doseur' is in charge of the 'liqueur d'expedition' the final magician's brew prior to shipment. For the vintage

45

dry blends Brut/Nature or Extra Dry/Sec/Très Sec the Grand Marques dosage produces the following usual degrees of dryness (i.e. of sugar content):

Krug	½–¾%
Bollinger	½–¾%
Pol Roger	1¼%
Moet & Chandon	1½%
Lanson	1¾%

For non-vintage popular blends the dosage will be fractionally higher.

●The Chef de Chantier of 'Boucleur' is in charge of the driving-in of the characteristic shaped branded cork.

●The 'Ficeleur' is in charge of capping and wiring each bottle.

Label clues

The small print on the label tells you a great deal. The shipper, the region, the style (Sec etc.) The letters NM stand 'for 'negociant-manipulant' a term for either merchant or shipper, as are the vast majority of firms in the business. RM stands for 'recoltant-manipulant' who are the small vigneron growers. M stands for 'co-operative-manipulant' who are the large wine co-operatives grouping the smaller vignerons together, who do not have the capital or expertise to bottle and ship direct to the customers. MA stands for 'marque d'acheteur' or Buyers Own Brand (known as B.O.B. in the trade). Large wine merchants or supermarket chains in this country have a possible option to purchase under their own label or brand i.e. Sainsbury, Tesco, etc.

The champagne wine pressure in the bottle is equivalent to 6 kilos per square centimetre compared to 3 or 4 kg. pressure for the 'Crémants' — sparkling wines of Burgundy and Alsace. Champagne has larger bubbles than the 'creaming' Crémants. Wines which are made from the white Chardonnay grapes only, are labelled Blanc de Blancs.

Rosé champagnes can be made in two quite different ways. The village of Bouzy produces still *red* wine and this is added to the young wine during the blending after the first fermentation and before bottling. The other method is for the two black skinned grapes, Pinot Noir and Pinot Meunier, to be left in contact ('maceration') with the initial grape 'must' thus producing a pale rose coloured wine with a gooseberry flavour.

The local still wines cannot be called champagne, but have their own red or white Appellation Controlée called 'Coteau Champenois'. Remember that 'La Champagne' is the name of the region and 'Le Champagne' is the name of the sparkling A.C. wine!

A good wine shipper's blended cuvée would be as follows:—

- *Black grapes*
  Verzenay 10%, Bouzy 10%, Ay 10%, Pierry 10%, Vertus 10%, Chigny 5% and Champillon 5%. Total 60%.

- *White grapes*
  Cramant/Avize 20%, Le Mesnil 10%, Chouilly 5% and Crayons de St. Martin 5%. Total 40%.

Many of the better and richer champagne shippers put aside each year a reserve of 1% or more in magnums into stock as a buffer against a poor vintage. Total stocks in the region are estimated at over 700 million bottles or just over three years sales, but the Co-ops and MR's have almost six years supply in stock.

Relatively few champagne merchants actually own more than token vineyards. These include Bollinger whose 270 acres produce 70% of their annual requirements and Roederer, Tattinger and Henriot who also own vineyards.

Some more facts and figures

There are 15,000 individual champagne vignerons owning their own vineyards.

8,000 have *less* than 1 hectare (2½ acres)
3,000 have between 1–2 hectares
3,200 have between 2–5 hectares

47

Structure of the industry

It is very rare to find a vigneron owning/farming more than 5 hectares (12½ acres). Each hectare produces up to 50 hectolitres of wine. Nearly half (48%) of the total production is sold as grapes to the merchant houses or co-operatives. A typical small wine farmer with say 1 hectare of vines will earn about £10,000 gross (5,000 litres @ 22 francs per litre).

There are 130 wine co-operatives grouping 10,700 small vignerons together who own 10,400 hectares (just less than 1 hectare each). There are 11 co-operative unions some of whom are very powerful and market their finished product under Buyers Own Brands.

The 110 champagne shippers own 3,200 hectares of vineyards and the nine largest shippers own between them 2,500 hectares. The shippers account for 65% of the annual champagne shipments and the growers 33%. (The co-operatives 6% and the Récoltants Manipulants 27% of the total). The Récoltants sell locally to shops, cafés, restaurants and friends — and of course, drink their own liquid gold themselves!

Employment statistics

The champagne trade employs over 30,000 people as follows:

In the vineyards

14,300 working vineyard owners

5,500 salaried vineyard owners (mainly with the big negociants)

500 salaried personnel on the books of the Co-operatives

On the commercial side

1,300 employed selling, maintaining vine products and equipment.

3,400 employed working in the caves and chais

1,400 employed in office work

Additionally

150 courtiers & agents selling wines or holding stocks

100 employed by the several champagne associations

4,500 salaried personnel in anciliary trades — bottles, bottling plants, casks.

Major players

The ten champagne groups who account for 80% of the negociant market are, in order of importance:

1. Moet-Hennessy including Moet et Chandon, Mercier and Ruinart.
2. Seagram group including Mumm, Heidsieck-Monopole and Perrier-Jouet.
3. BSN French group including Lanson and Pommery.
4. Veuve Cliquot-Ponsardin, Canard Duchene and Henriot.
5. Laurent Perrier and Lemoine.
6. Tattinger and Irroy.
7. Remy Martin Group including Charles Heidsieck and Krug.
8. Marne et Champagne.
9. Piper Heidsieck.
10. Louis Roederer.

Medium sized firms

The next group is of medium sized shippers who account for 15% of the negociant market with annual sales each between half a million and 2½ million bottles. Ayala/Montbello, Abele, Besserat de Bellefon/Salon, Billecart Salmon, Boizel, Bollinger, Bricout, De Castellane, Charbout, Deutz & Geldermann, Duval Leroy, H. Germain, Gosset & Philliponat, Chateau Lafitte, Joseph Perrier, Pol Roger, Rapaneau & Martel, Same & Marie-Stuart and De Venoge & Troillard. The remaining 70 negociant-shippers account for 5% of the negociant market i.e. approximately 6-7 million bottles between them.

Luxury product

Champagne is expensive. The price paid to growers for their grapes is twice that of Burgundy or Alsace, less than 100 miles away. The similar soil, with the same grapes, using the same 'Methode Champenoise' production methods produce a very good sparkling wine at 40% of the champagne price.

There are a variety of reasons for the disparity in prices. The vignerons in Champagne receive prices for their grapes often *ten* times more expensive than for grapes grown in most other areas of France. The C.I.V.C. (Comité Interprofessionnel du Vin du Champagne) in Epernay was formed in 1944 under the auspices of the French Ministry of Agriculture and Viticulture. It performs a delicate balancing trick co-ordinating the interest of the many thousands of individual vineyard owners with the negociant merchant shippers and the co-operatives. Quality control (not more than 50 hectolitres per hectare), advice and monitoring of every facet in the trade are also their responsibility. They have the task of rating each individual wine commune into various 'crûs'. The top 'crû' receives a 100% grading and 100% of that year's price per kilo of grapes. For instance the poor little Aube growers will get about 75%, those in the Aisne 75–82% and in the Marne from 75–100%. The top grade crûs called 'Hors Classe' are at Ambonnay, Avize, Ay, Beaumont sur Vesle, Bouzy, Chouilly (white), Cramant, Louvois, Le Mesnil sur Oger, Oger, Oiry, Mailly, Puisieulx, Sillery, Tours sur Marne (black), Verzy and Verzenay.

The annual assessment is called the 'Echelle'. The kilo price in 1962 was 3.25 francs and remained so for four years. Since then it has crept up inexorably. Occasionally a freak production year will see a sudden leap up (or down — 1975, 1983 and more recently in 1986 and 1987). It is now 21.77 francs per kilo! I know that excellent vineyards in the south, south west and south east of France are still receiving 3 or 4 francs per kilo or less! Some of these wines are much better than the *still* champagne wine! Nevertheless, the champagne shippers' overheads are very high. Stock averages 3 – 4 years sales and this is a costly investment.

The problem is that although the large French market now buys 120–130 million bottles a year, exports to the rest of the world, including the UK, continue to increase to well over 70 million bottles. For the first time ever, total shipments of all champagne topped 218 million bottles in 1987. So that the dangerous equation of annual sales = annual production very nearly exists. Dangerous because of the temptation to growers, negociants, importers and retailers to price up still quicker! There are 14,000 wine growers and 100 shipping houses. Altogether over 30,000 people work in the champagne industry. It is one of the most prosperous areas in France as a result.

Family heritage

The earliest negociant wine shippers were Ruinart which was started on 1st September 1729, almost by mistake, by a cloth merchant called Nicholas Ruinart of Epernay who later moved to Reims. In 1743 Claude Louis Nicolas Moet founded his firm. A Francis Delamotte and a Monsieur Lanson were partners in 1750. When the last Delamotte died in 1838 the firm became simply Lanson Père. A Monsieur Clicquot founded a champagne firm in 1772; he married a Mademoiselle Ponsardin of Reims in 1794. Several German families came to Reims, Avize and Ay such as Florenz Heidsieck who was trading at Reims in 1785, joined by his nephew Charles in 1805. Of the three Heidsieck firms now trading, only Charles' firm is owned by the original family. Moet & Chandon were partners and brothers in law in 1832.

Festivals in Champagne

The Saint Vincent wine festival of vignerons is celebrated throughout France including the Champagne area on 22nd January or the Sunday nearest to that date. It cheers up the hard, cold winter days and whole villages take part. An unofficial festival is called Cochelet, celebrated by the small family vignerons as a kind of harvest festival in late October. In midsummer the wine festival of St. Jean on 24th June or the nearest Saturday and the Wine Fairs at Bar sur Aube take place on the second Sunday in September. Reims and Epernay have several other wine 'manifestations' throughout the year.

On your travels look out for the vineyards with peculiar names. For instance, Côte aux Enfants, Voie aux Vaches, Champ du Clerc, Faubourg d'Enfer (Hell!), Les Gouttes d'Or, Les Aumonières, Pisse-Renard (yes, it does mean what you think) and Froid-Cul.

CHAPTER SIX:
CHAMPAGNE HOUSES

Reims

Reims has no less than 37 champagne houses, as does Epernay. Those in Reims (telephone code 26) are now listed in alphabetical order with some notes about each one.

●*Besserat de Bellefon,* Allée du Vignoble, 36 09 18.
Visits by appointment but a one hour tour with tasting is possible. Now owned by the huge Pernod Ricard group, Besserat, who were founded in 1843 specialise in crémants, a light champagne style. Total sales rather under 200,000 cases. Try their Crémant des Moines rosé.

●*Charles Heidsieck,* 3 Place des Droits de l'Homme, 85 03 27.
Closed in August, visits by appointment. Founded in 1851, now owned by the large Cognac group Remy Martin who also own Krug champagne. Annual sales 300,000 cases. Try their 1979 Vintage Cuvée Champagne Charlie. They also produce a local still wine, Cuvée des Augustins and a Marc de Champagne.

●*George Goulet,* 4 Avenue du General Giraud, 85 05 77.
Visits by appointment. Founded in 1834.

●*Heidsieck Monopole,* 83 rue Coquebert, 07 39 34.
Visits by appointment. Founded in 1785, they introduced their famous Dry Monopole brand in 1860. Now owned by the powerful Seagram group who also own G.H. Mumm and Perrier Jouet. They produce 150,000 cases a year and own 85 hectares mainly at Verzenay. My family port wine

shippers shared UK agents with Heidsieck so we have been drinking their Monopole Brut for many years.

●*Henriot & Co.,* 6 Avenue du General Giraud, 61 14 14.
It is now linked with Veuve Clicquot Ponsardin. Founded in 1808, they own 103 hectares and produce 100,000 cases annually. Their expensive Reserve Champagne is called Baron Phillippe de Rothschild.

●*André Jacquart,* 5 rue Gosset.
This is a substantial C.R.V.C. co-operative whose members own 1,000 hectares and produce two thirds of a million cases each year, of which one sixth of a million go under the Jacquart name.

●*Krug,* 5 rue Coquebert, 88 24 24.
Closed in July. Visits by appointment. Founded in 1843, they produce only 40,000 cases a year of the finest champagne in the world! Try their famous Grande Cuvée.

●*Lanson Père et Fils,* 12 Boulevard Lundy, 40 36 26.
Visits by appointment. Founded in 1760, now owned by the huge French group BSN who also own Pommeroy. Lanson have 200 hectares of vineyards and produce half a million cases. Try their Black Label Brut.

●*Abel Lepitre,* 2–4 Avenue de General Giraud, 85 05 77.
Closed in August and weekends. Visits by appointment. A small firm linked with George Goulet and Saint Marceaux. Sales about 50,000 cases a year.

●*G. H. Mumm,* 29 rue du Champ de Mars, 40 22 73.
Open to visitors without appointment except weekends. Ask for Madame Loilier. Founded in 1827, they have 220 hectares of vineyards, now owned by Seagram. Try their Cordon Rouge Brut with its scarlet band across the label. Mumm are probably No. 2 to Moet & Chandon in size. Huge caves.

53

●*Piper Heidsieck,* 51 Boulevard Henry Vasnick, 85 01 94.
Visits all the year round. Their electric train will take you through their caves. Founded in 1834, they make nearly half a million cases annually. Very popular in the European royal courts. Still privately owned and produce good vintage wines.

●*Pommery & Greno,* 5 Place du General Gouraud, 05 05 01.
Open to visits all the year round. Founded in 1836, they own 300 hectares and produce nearly half a million cases annually. Now, like Lanson, owned by the French BSN group. Probably the most elegant tour of any houses in their 18 km. of galleries.

●*Louis Roederer,* 21 Boulevard Lundy, 40 42 11.
Closed in July. Visits by appointment. Founded in 1776, they own nearly 200 hectares of vineyards and produce 200,000 cases. Famed as a real quality house, their vintage wines are highly regarded. Try their Cristal Roederer Champagne.

●*Ruinart,* 4 rue les Crayères, 85 40 29.
Weekday visits by appointment. Founded in 1729, Ruinart are the oldest champagne house. Now owned, like Moet & Chandon, by the Moet-Hennessy Cognac group. They own 15 hectares of vineyards and produce 100,000 cases each year. Try their Dom Ruinart, named after Dom Perignon's friend and colleague.

●*Taittinger,* 9 Place St. Nicase, 85 45 35.
Open all the year for visits except Saturdays. Founded as recently as 1930, they have 240 hectares of vineyards and produce a third of a million cases annually. Taittinger own Ernest Irroy, an older, smaller champagne house. Their caves were once part of an abbey.

●*Veuve Clicquot Ponsardin,* 1 Place des Droits de l'Homme, 85 24 08.
Closed in August but open the rest of the year for visits. In

winter months best ring or write for appointments. Founded in 1772, thus one of the earliest shippers. The famous 'widow' was Madame Ponsardin who married Francois Clicquot in 1799. They produce 600,000 cases a year mostly in their bright orange label and own 270 hectares of vineyards. Try their rich fruity Yellow Label Clicquot Brut.

Other Reims shippers include Henri Abele (63,000 cases). Marie Stuart (100,000 cases), Montaudon (40,000 cases), Bruno Paillard (20,000 cases).

Epernay

Epernay (telephone code 25) has an equally distinguished collection of champagne shippers — again in alphabetical order.

●*Beaumet,* 3 rue Malakoff, 54 53 34.
Linked with Oudinot and Jeanmaire.

●*Boizel,* 14/16 rue de Bernon, 55 21 51.
Founded in 1834 and produces 80,000 cases including the Kremer brand.

●*Ellner,* 1 rue Côte Legris, 53 20 25.
Visits by appointment.

●*De Castellane,* 57 rue de Verdun, 55 15 33.
Open all the year round but October-April by appointment. Production under 200,000 cases. Look for the tower, 237 steps up, with the red cross on it. Also own Maxims brand of champagne and a champagne museum.

●*Charles de Cazanove,* 1 rue des Cotelles.
Produce 12,500 cases each year.

●*A. Charbaut & Fils,* 17 Avenue de Champagne, 54 37 55.
Founded in 1948 at Mareuil sur Ay. Own 56 hectares of vineyards and produce 150,000 cases each year. Visits by groups only.

●*A. Desmoulins,* 44 Avenue Foch, 54 24 24.
Founded in 1908 and produce 12,500 cases each year.

●*Alfred Gratien,* 30 rue Maurice Cerveaux, 54 38 20.
Owned by the Seydoux family of Saumur. Founded in 1864,
they produce 12,500 cases.

●*Marne & Champagne,* 22 rue Maurice Cerveaux, 54 21 66.
This is a huge firm which (a) supplies other shippers, (b) is big
in B.O.B. brands and (c) has launched Eugène Cliquot,
Alfred Rothschild and Giesler brands.

●*Mercier,* 73 Avenue de Champagne, 54 75 26.
Visits all the year round. Founded in 1858, has huge cellars
18 km. long and is part of the Moet & Chandon/Hennessy
group. They own 200 hectares of vineyards and produce
one third of a million cases each year. Used to have a cheap
and cheerful image. A tour will probably include a free glass!

●*Miltat,* 72 Avenue Foch, 54 09 74.
Open for visits and tastings.

●*Moet et Chandon,* 18 Avenue de Champagne, 54 71 11.
Open all the year with sophisticated tours of 45 minutes.
Look at the statue of the monk Dom Perignon in the
courtyard. Founded in 1743 they own 460 hectares and
produce a staggering 2 million cases a year, easily the largest
'negociant'. There is a wine museum open to the public in
their huge offices. An essential visit by all travellers to
Champagne country. A tour will probably include a free
glass!

●*Oudinot,* 12 rue Godart Roger, 54 60 31.
Founded in 1889, they own 62 hectares of vineyards and
produce 40,000 cases each year. They are linked with
Chateau Jeanmaire and Chateau Beaumet.

●*Perrier Jouet,* 24–28 Avenue de Champagne, 55 20 53.
Visits by appointment only. Probably the smartest champagne

brand over the last century (founded 1811) and drunk by Sarah Bernhardt and Queen Victoria. They own 40 hectares of vineyards and produce a quarter of a million cases each year. Like Mumm and Heidsieck Monopole, they are now owned by Seagram. A fashionable and a quality brand.

●*Pol Roger,* 1 rue Henri Lelarge, 55 41 95.
Closed in August but open to visits the rest of the year. Founded in 1849 the firm is still family owned. They have 70 hectares of vineyards and ship rather over 100,000 cases each year. Sir Winston Churchill's favourite bubbly and very popular in the UK. Try their vintage and rosé champagnes. Again, a fashionable and a quality brand.

●*Rapeneau,* 69 Avenue de Champagne.
Produces 125,000 cases a year and own the Martel trade name. Also at 4 rue Paul Bert in Magenta.

●*S. A. Magenta-Epernay,* 1 rue des Cotelles, 54 23 46.
Founded in 1920, owned by the Lombard family. They make almost 200,000 cases each year, mainly B.O.B. brands.

●*J. de Telmont,* 1 Avenue de Champagne.
Founded in 1920 and owns 24 hectares. Sales about 25,000 cases a year.

●*Venoge,* 30 Avenue de Champagne, 55 01 01.
Open for visits to their splendid offices and chais. Founded in 1837 they sell 100,000 cases a year. Try their vintage Champagne des Princes.

Champagne growers in the Aube

Very few people know about this area which is 100 miles south of Reims and is planted with 4,800 hectares (12,000 acres) of vineyards, or nearly one fifth of the total in Champagne. The area stretches from just north of the old town of Bar sur Aube, across country to Essoyes and Bar sur

Seine to Les Riceys on the northern border with Burgundy. Another small vineyard area is to be found on the chalk ridge of Montgeux just west of Troyes. Before the wholesale Phylloxera destruction at the end of the 19th century no less than 57,000 acres of vineyards were planted. After replanting the Pinot Noir was replaced with the Gamay grape which gave a better yield at the expense of quality. In the 1950's the Gamay was uprooted and replaced with Pinot Noir. The topsoil is very stony and the stones retain the heat to warm the vine roots. The vineyards are planted on steep southern facing hillsides, particularly in the Seine Valley. The 100 mile distance from Reims produces a warmer summer and better harvests.

In the area are 2,200 wine growers, but only 375 produce a champagne. Côteaux Champenois is made here and Les Riceys produces a notable still rosé wine. At the vintage 45% of the grapes are made into champagne locally and 55% are bought by the major champagne houses around Reims and Epernay. A total of 9 million bottles of champagne are made each year in the Aube. A recent trade promotion in London showed the champagne wines of a score of Aube producers. I tasted most of them and at least half I thought were remarkably good value. They are all relatively small family owned shippers, some founded between the World Wars with landholding in the 7–15 hectare range. Some of them have agents in the UK but the majority are looking for agents and importers.

- *Michel Baujean,* la Mansardiere, Bagneux la Fosse, 10340 Les Riceys. 25 29 37 44.
  Founded 1953, has 15 hectares of vineyards, sells 7,000 cases per annum.

- *Cheurlin & Fils,* 13 rue de la Gare, Gyé sur Seine, 10250 Mussy sur Seine. 25 38 20 27.
  Founded 1958, has 22 hectares of vineyards, sells 10,000 cases per annum.

- *A. Drappier,* Urville, 10200 Bar sur Aube. 25 26 40 15.
  Founded 1950, has 27 hectares of vineyards, sells 10–12,000 cases per annum.

●*Robert Dufour & Fils,* 4 rue de la Croix Malot, Landreville, 10110 Bar sur Seine. 25 38 52 25.
Founded 1925, has 9 hectares, sells 5,000 cases per annum.

●*Fleury,* Courteron, 10250 Mussy sur Seine. 25 38 23 54.
Founded 1895, has 12 hectares, makes 6,000 cases per annum.

●*G. Fontaine,* le Moulin, Balnot sur Laignes, 10110 Bar sur Seine. 25 29 31 87.
Côteaux Champenois wines as well. Founded 1974, has 5 hectares, sells 3,000 cases per annum.

●*Gauthrin Laurent,* Bligny, 10200 Bar sur Aube. 25 26 45 83.
Founded 1900, has 5 hectares of vineyards, sells 2,500 cases per annum.

●*Christian Lassoigne-Berlot,* Montgueux, 10300 Sainte Savine 25 74 84 60.
Founded 1970, has 5 hectares, sells 2,500 cases per annum.

●*René Chuillier,* Fontette, 10350 Essoyes. 25 29 61 80.
Founded 1900, has 15 hectares, sells 10,000 cases per annum. Creme de Cassis & Framboise as well.

●*Michel Noirot,* Clos St. Roch, 4 Avenue de la Croix Mission, 10340 Les Riceys. 25 29 38 46.
Founded 1966, has 10½ hectares, sells 8,000 cases per annum.

●*Bernard Robert Voigny,* 10202 Bar sur Aube. 25 27 11 53.
Founded 1945, has 22 hectares, makes 12,000 cases per annum.

●*Christian Senez,* Fontette, 10360 Essoyes. 25 29 60 62.
Côteaux Champenois wines as well.

●*Treuffet, Père et Fils,* Balnot sur Laignes, 10110 Bar sur Seine. 25 29 38 73.

●*Marcel Vezten,* Celles sur Ource, 10110 Bar sur Seine.
25 38 50 22.
Founded 1900, has 10 hectares, sells 8,000 cases per annum.

●*Herard & Fluteau,* Gye sur Seine, 10250 Mussy sur Seine.
25 38 20 02.
Founded 1935, has 7 hectares. Represented by K. F. Butler Limited of East Grinstead.

●*Alexandre Bonnet,* 138 rue General de Gaulle, 10340 Les Riceys. 25 29 30 93.

●*Serge Mathieu,* Avirey Lingeny, 10340 Les Riceys.
25 29 32 58.
Founded 1900, has 10 hectares, sells 5,000 cases per annum.

Two other shippers in the Aube are:
●*Jean Arnoult,* 86 Grande Rue, 10110 Celles sur Ource,
25 38 50 06.

●*Francois Diligent,* Buxeuil, 10110 Bar sur Seine.
25 38 50 76.

A wine tour is shown in the Aube departement. (Chapter Thirteen).

Aisne

The Aisne departement has several champagne houses.

●*Baron Albert of Porteron,* 02310 Charly sur Marne.
23 82 02 65.
They have been wine growers since 1677! Porteron is in the bend of the River Marne on the D969 south west of Chateau Thierry. Visits by arrangement.

●*Pannier,* 23 rue Roger Catillon, 02400 Chateau Thierry.
23 69 13 10.
This is rather larger and accepts visits without notice.

Other Aisne champagne shippers are:
- *Michel Henry,* of Mont Sainte Père.

- *Lafleur-Julien,* Marcilly, 02130 Barzy sur Marne.
  12 70 22 54.

- *Alain Bedel,* Porterons, Charly sur Marne. 23 82 02 74.

- *Derot Delugny,* 16–21 Grande Rue, Crouttes sur Marne, 02310 Charly. 23 70 02 14.

- *Veuve Olivier & Fils,* Trelon sur Marne. 23 70 24 01.

- *Michel Boilleau,* 02560 Fossay.

There are 2,200 hectares of vineyards in the Aisne or 8% of the total under cultivation. The total stock of champagne in the Aisne caves amounts to 5 million bottles, with average annual sales of 12–15,000 cases, Les Caves Pannier being the largest. The association is called Co-operateurs de Champagne, Avenue Ernest Couvrecelle, 02400 Etampes sur Marne (23 70 76 76). Le Pinot Noir is the predominant variety of grape. The helpful tourist office, Place de l'Hotel de Ville in Chateau Thietry will arrange vineyard tours.

Agencies are available in U.K. from Champagne Agencies Ltd., 23, Kings Road, Windsor, Berkshire SL4 2AD. Tel 0753 854329.

Harvesting the champagne crop

CHAPTER SEVEN: WINE TOURS

Local champagne wine tours in the Marne

The tourist office in Epernay, 7 Avenue de Champagne, tel. (prefix 26) 55 33 00 is run by a charming, most efficient and helpful lady. The bureau have devised three delightful wine tours which are briefly described in this chapter — all starting from Epernay. The wine villages are described in more detail in a later chapter.

There are three categories of visits. The really large sophisticated firms mainly in Reims or Epernay, accept guided visits without notice and are open all the year. Tasting facilities vary and one is not necessarily expected to purchase your host's wines. The second category is of good quality medium sized firms who need warning by letter or telephone in advance of a meeting and visit. A small purchase would be appreciated but is not required. The third category is of visits to the very small vigneron-shippers and it would be uncharitable to come away empty handed as the proprietor himself will probably take time off to show you round.

Those firms in italics are either very large or relatively large, whose quality is known at first hand to the author. The serious tasting visitor to the region would be advised to set up a meeting beforehand, either through the UK agent or major retail customer, or locally through the tourist office in Epernay by telephone. Each tour will take a morning or afternoon drive depending, of course, on the number of visits made to growers and chais. (I suggest the purchase of Michelin Map No. 56 which will make the tour much easier for the car driver).

Tour number one

La Montagne de Reims. This is the northern tour. Take the N51 towards Reims, cross the River Marne and turn first right on the D1 road signed for Ay, which is the third most important champagne name after Reims and Epernay. The two very big names here are *Bollinger* (tel. 26 50 12 34) and *Ayala* (tel. 26 55 15 44), but visits have to be by appointment. Both are closed at weekends and Bollinger in August. The smaller firms are Deutz, 16 rue Jeanson, and Collery (who charge 6 francs per person), René Brun and Guy Dauby. Also there are Gosset, R. Goutorbe, Gatinois (Cheval Pierre), Ivergel and Fliniaux. The Association Co-operative de Viticulteurs de Premiers Crûs de la Marne is in the centre square, Place de la Liberation, tel. 26 50 11 95.

Keep eastwards to Mareuil sur Ay where *Philipponnat*, a quality house are based. Visits by appointment, not weekends or in August. Also Billecart Salmon. A smaller firm is R. Bernard, 21 rue du Corbier. Keep on to Bisseuil, Tours sur Marne where *Laurent Perrier*, tel. 26 58 91 22, is situated. Visits by appointment, not weekends or August, a big firm founded in 1812, owns 850 hectares and produces two thirds of a million cases a year. A. Chauvet, tel. 26 59 92 47, visits by appointment.

Next east to Condé, north to Ambonnay on the D37, and Bouzy D19, two very well known quality villages and north west on the D34 to Louvois. Just north east of Ambonnay is Trepail where G. Maizières, 1 rue du Stade welcomes visits (tel. 26 57 05 04). From Louvois, south west on the D9 to Tauxières Mutry, Fontaines sur Ay, Avenay and Mutigny to Ay once again.

Keep on the N51 north west to Dizy and up the steep hill at Champillon. Just 10 km. north east is Rilly la Montagne where Adam Garnotel, 17 rue de Chigny, tel. 26 03 40 22, will welcome you. The much larger Producteurs *Mailly*, tel. 26 49 41 10, will welcome you every day — free of charge, but times of entry vary. The prestigious *Canard Duchêne* are in Ludes on the D26 near Rilly la Montagne and they are open during the week and in August. Visits without prior warning.

Next door to the north west is Cormicy village with Cantoni

Guerlet, 16 rue la President Kennedy, tel. 26 61 31 58, open for visits. Back on the circuit south west on the D386 to Hautvillers (Dom Perignon's village) where Lopez Martin, Les Côtes de l'Hery, tel. 26 59 42 17 are open for visits, and then back via Cumières and Magenta to Epernay. In Magenta are Rapeneau, 4 rue Bert and Sacotte, 13 rue de la Verrerie.

Tour number two

The second wine tour is towards la Côte des Blancs, south of Epernay. Initially east on the D3 signed for Chalons to Chouilly where Hostomme & Fils, 5 rue de l'Allée, tel. 26 55 40 79 will welcome you. A minor road south east from Chouilly takes you to the hamlet of Cuis to Le Brun et Fils, 17 route d'Epernay, tel. 26 55 12 35.

Then south east on the D10 to Cramant, which has an unusual Menhir (huge man placed stone) 'de Haute Borne' and a vigneron co-operative. It is the northernmost of four important quality wine growing villages of Cramant, Avize, Oger and le Mesnil sur Oger, all on the D19. At Avize (population 1,700) there is the wine college (Ecole de Viticulture et d'Oenologie); Charles de Bigault, 26 rue Pasteur, A. Bricout & Koch, 7 rue de Cramant and Yve Lanaud, 3 Place Leon Bourgeois. Oger has F. Bonnet. These villages produce top quality grapes.

In Le Mesnil there are five producers.

A. *Jacquart* (see Reims), Salon Le Mesnil, D. Pertois, Robert Alain and B. Launois all in the Avenue de la Republique. M. Rocourt is at 1 rue des Zalieux. All welcome visits. Launois welcome groups and have a champagne museum. Also visit the Robert Billion co-operative. On the same D9, 5.5 kms. south is Vertus. *Duval Leroy,* rue du Mont Chenil is a substantial firm. Champagne Napoleon needs advance warning, tel. 26 52 11 74. Champagne M. Rogue, 15 rue du Gal Leclerc, tel. 26 52 15 68 is open to visits, so too are A. Prieur and Lafitte. Keep south for 4 km. to Bergeres les Vertus and spare a few minutes to visit the Chateau de la Reine Blanche on Mont Aime. Although a ruin, there is a marvellous view from the 237 metre high hill.

The wine circuit continues west on the D33 to Etoges, where there is a chateau and south on a minor road to Congy where Breton et Fils, 12 rue Courte Pilate, tel. 26 59 31 03 will welcome you. Courjeonnet is 3 km. due south to see there Ragot Nomine, tel. 26 59 31 57. Head due west on to the main Epernay — Sezanne road, the D51 and turn north through Baye (a chateau) Champaubert and 6 km. to Montmort Lucy. Here Breton et Fils in the hamlet of Longy will welcome you any day of the week as will Nomine Renard in the hamlet of Villevenard, tel. 26 59 16 13.

Then keep on the D51 for 15 km. north east towards Epernay. Visit too the Co-operative de Mancy, tel. 26 59 71 52. Stop to see the chateau at Brugny, D. Frezier, 8 rue G. Poittevin in Monthelon, tel. 26 59 70 16 and Duverger Père et Fils, 15 rue du Champagne in Moussy, tel. 26 54 03 54. Crete Pertois is also in Moussy, 15 Avenue du Mont Felix, tel. 26 54 03 63. The final port of call is at Pierry in the southern outskirts of Epernay at *P. Gobillard,* 43 rue Leon Bourgeois, tel. 26 54 05 11. The chais are in the Chateau de Pierry.

Tour number three

The final wine tour out of Epernay is westwards to Vallée de la Marne, starting on the N3. In Mardeuil 2 km. along are C. Dubois, rue Paul Langevin, tel. 26 55 25 65 and Gaillot et Fils, 12 rue de la Liberte, tel. 26 55 31 42. Keep west through Vauciennes to Boursault (both on a minor road south and parallel to the N3). J. Berat is in rue Saint Roch, tel. 26 58 42 45. In the next two little villages to the west are producers Rasselet Père et Fils, 18 rue des Hussards in Montvoisin Oeuilly, tel. 26 58 30 26 and Tarlant, 55 rue de la Co-operative in Oeuilly, tel. 26 58 40 60. Now head south west on the D423 to Festigny to see H. Loriot, 13 rue Bel Air, tel. 26 58 33 44. A detour perhaps 10 km. south to see P. Mignon, rue des Grappes d'Or in Le Breuil, tel. 26 59 22 03.

Just north of Festigny is the village of Port a Binson. Cross over the River Marne into Chatillon sur Marne. There *Jackie Charlier,* 4 rue des Pervenches (Montigny sous Chatillon), tel. 26 58 35 18, will give you a professional guided tour and tasting. Closed during vintage time and the last fortnight in August.

Just 2 km. west of Chatillon sur Marne is Vandières where there are three small producers. D. Moreau, rue du Moulin, tel. 26 58 01 64; B. Nowack, 15 rue Bailly, tel. 26 58 02 69 and Delabarre Brochet, 26 rue de Chatillon, tel. 26 58 02 65. A kilometre to the east of Chatillon is J. Charpentier, rue de Reuil in Villers sous Chatillon, tel. 26 58 05 78.

Keep east along the D1 running parallel to the Marne via Venteuil where there is a monument to the English army dead and via the D22 to Fleury la Rivière to see Pommelet at 4 rue des Longschamp, tel. 26 58 41 04 and then back via Domery and Cumières on the D1 and across the river back into Epernay. You will see the delightful hotel/restaurant la Terrasse on your right near the bridge who will offer you an excellent meal and a coup de champagne at a reasonable price. You have almost certainly earned it!

Other villages within reach of Epernay also harbour champagne negociants.

Avize. Union Champagne, 7 rue Pasteur, a huge co-operative with 1,000 member vignerons, producing 400,000 cases each year. Look for their St. Gall brand.

Ambonnay. A. Secondé Prevoteau, 2 rue du Chateau who own 12 hectares.

Bouzy. Talleyrand, the diplomatic fox of Europe in the early 19th century, called the Bouzy *red* champagne the 'vin de civilisation.' In the village is a major co-operative. May is the best month to see the wide variety of iris growing here.

Chalons sur Marne. Albert le Brun, 93 Avenue de Paris was founded in 1860. They produce 30,000 cases a year, look for .their Blanc de Blancs Brut. Also visit Joseph Perrier, 69 Avenue de Paris, founded in 1825 who now make 55,000 cases each year and are getting known in the UK.

Chateau Thierry (Aisne). To the west of Epernay. Pannier, 23 rue Roger Catillon make 170,000 cases each year.

Cumières. Leclerc Briant founded in 1872 make 25,000 cases a year.

Cramant. Bonnaire, 105 rue de Carrouge produce Champagne de Cramant.

Magenta. Sacotte, 13 rue de la Verrerie were founded in 1887 and make 25,000 cases each year.

Rilly la Montagne. Mailly Champagne were founded in 1920. A well known co-operative with 70 hectares of vineyards, producing 40,000 cases annually.

Tours sur Marne. Barancourt own 50 hectares of vineyards and produce 50,000 cases each year. They also make still red Côteaux Champenois wine.

Vaudemange. Chaldron Guerin et Fils own 15 hectares of vineyards and produce 13,000 cases each year.

Vertus. Vranken-Lafitte of Le Pave, founded in 1976, sell Veuve Monnier and Charles Lafitte brands, altogether 110,000 cases.

My personal advice is that if you are spending a few days based in or near Epernay, as soon as you arrive, make an appointment to visit Bollinger, Ayala, Philipponnat and Canard Duclerc. These are high class shippers with excellent quality wines. Before and after visits/tours wander round the charming countryside. The dozens of small villages are described in another chapter — churches, chateaux, museums and those with an interesting historical legacy. Note that the small town of Ay houses a dozen shippers, some with eminent names. Finally see Chapter Fourteen for champagne wine tours in the Aube departement.

CHAPTER EIGHT:
THE CHAMPAGNE EXPRESS

There is a long history of British connection with Champagne, the wine and the region. Indeed, for most years Britain was the leading export market for champagne and is still regarded by the Champenois as the benchmark for international markets.

The following are examples of that long history:

- In 1359, during the Hundred Years War with France, Edward III arrived in Reims intent on having himself crowned King of France. However, both he and his army were driven back by the French.

- When Henry VII landed in France in 1495, the vignerons near Reims were ordered to pull up their vines for fear that the British would use them for cooking or for filling moats to scale the city walls.

- In the reign of Henry VIII, Admiral Bonnivet wrote in 1518 to Cardinal Wolsey advising him that 20 'poincons de vin d'Ay' were being shipped to him.

- Henry VIII bought vineyards in the region in the 16th century where he had his own presses and envoys to produce wines from Champagne for the English court. The King had his own broker in Ay to secure the best wines available.

- In 1622 the Marquis de Saint-Evremond fell into disgrace in the French Court so sought refuge in the English Court, where he re-introduced the courtesans to the delights of the Sillery wines of Champagne. He became a favourite of our

Dutch King, William III, who however preferred still red champagne wine.

- Roger l'Estranges' 1664 edition of Butlers Hudibras has the magic lines "Drink every letter o'it in stun, and make it brisk champagne become".

- In 1667/8 Mr. Batailley, personal friend of Samuel Pepys (and his Huguenot wife) supplied wines not only to the Pepys but to Lord Crofts for fine champagne wine of Sillery.

- Bertin du Rocheret of Ay knew many Jacobin exiles and they persuaded their friends in London c.1720 to buy his sparkling champagne wines and appointed an agent, a M. Chabane. Later the first three King George's all tried, tasted and liked the sparkling wine.

- In 1806 the Prince Regent ordered 2,000 bottles of the House of Sillery champagne, vintage 1802. It is believed that most of this went into the making of his favourite drink 'Regent's Punch'. During the same period, both Sheridan and Byron extolled the delights of champagne.

- Due to various duties on French wines, champagne was at this time very expensive (approximately eight shillings a bottle compared to port at two shillings a bottle). It was not until Gladstone negotiated a trade treaty with France for reduced duties on French wine that a bottle of champagne cost approximately five shillings.

- The British set the fashion for 'Brut' (dry) champagne and in 1830 Champagne Moet's first quality was advertised in the Times for 80 shillings a dozen.

- In 1869 the most popular music hall song was 'Champagne Charlie' sung by George Leyburn.

- In 1876 (sparkling) champagne was on sale in the Pleasure Gardens in Vauxhall. All the shippers declared an excellent

1874 vintage as Brut or Extra Dry selling at 71 shillings per case f.o.b. in 1880 (or 110 shillings in London).

● Edward VII, when out on a shoot, would be followed around by a boy carrying a basket full of bottles of champagne. When the King decided he would like a glass of champagne he would call up the boy and hence "a bottle of the boy" became as familiar an expression to the Edwardians as a bottle of bubbly is to ours. In the Gay Nineties the best vintages were 1892, 1893 and 1899.

● Sir Winston Churchill loved champagne — his favourite being Pol Roger — indeed he called his racehorse after it. He had a long and affectionate relationship with Maison Pol Roger and when he died, Madame Odette Pol Roger (the head of the House) ordered that a black border be put around the edge of their champagne label as a mark of respect and it remains today.

British connection

For many years the huge market in the UK for French champagne was dominated by the Champagne Academy — the leading negociant-shipping houses who proudly called themselves 'Hors Concours' (above competition). They are Bollinger, Charles Heidsieck, Heidsieck Dry Monopole, Krug, Lanson, Moet et Chandon, Mumm, Perrier-Jouet, Pol Roger, Pommery, Louis Roederer and Veuve Clicquot. For perhaps a hundred years these great names have reigned supreme and, of course, created our huge market.

However, their dominance has come under pressure from the major supermarket chains who now market their own brands of champagne seriously. For example, J. Sainsbury's launched in 1982 their Extra Dry blend made for them in Vertus and Sezanne by Duval Leroy. The top 15 brands in 1982 accounted for 5.2 million bottles or 67% of the UK champagne market. Five years later the same 15 top brands increased their sales dramatically to 9.1 million bottles but decreased their market share equally dramatically down to

56%. Soon the market of 20 million bottles will probably be split 55% between the very top 15 brands, perhaps 20–25% by the supermarket chains and 20–25% by the 70 or so smaller shippers involved in the UK market. J. Sainsbury launched their Pink Champagne in 1984 and their vintage champagne in 1986.

The next development was the entry of the major wine warehouses, selling by the case, with Majestic to the fore, which increased the overall market and took market share. The Oddbins chain, part of the Seagram group, has strongly promoted a range of champagnes, including G. H. Mumm, Heidsieck Monopole and Perrier-Jouet (also owned by Seagram). For most of the year Oddbins offer a free seventh bottle for every six bottles of champagne bought. They have certainly done their bit to increase sales in the High Street.

Market shares

Trade estimates of 20 million bottle sales currently in the UK market (the equivalent of 1,650,000 cases) is approximately as follows:

1. Supermarkets 250,000 cases.
J. Sainsbury, Marks & Spencer, Waitrose, Tesco, Safeway, Budgen, Asda, Liptons and Presto. My accolade goes to Waitrose who alone:
(a)   have a range of 12 Grande Marque brands as well as their own house brand
(b)   display all their champagnes *on their sides* for better conditioning of the wine.

2. Traditional markets.
Mostly through the big retail chains such as Oddbins, Victoria Wine, Unwins, Threshers, Peter Dominic, Bottoms Up, Augustus Barnet, the Co-op as well as the wine warehouses.

	Cases		Cases
Moet & Chandon	300,000	Taittinger	14,000
Lanson	130,000	Heidsieck Dry Monopole	13,000
G. H. Mumm	60,000	Ayala	13,000
Veuve Clicquot	53,000	Pol Roger	12,000
Bollinger	49,000	Bouche Père & Fils	9,000
Laurent Perrier	45,000	Pommery	8,000
Mercier	45,000	Canard Duchêne	7,000
Piper Heidsieck	38,000	Krug	7,000
A. Charbaut (BOB)	35,000	Perrier-Jouet	6,000
Charles Heidsieck	25,000	Joseph Perrier	5,000
Louis Roederer	14,000	Besserat de Bellefon	5,000

There are probably another hundred brands in the UK accounting for the remaining 300–400,000 cases. To name but a few who have a reputation for quality — J. de Telmont of Damery près Epernay, Philipponnat of Ay, Alfred Gratien and de Venoge.

3. Specialist importers

There are several small specialist importers of a *range* of champagnes who are doing a good job of educating the drinkers who know 'a little about champagne'.

(a) The Champagne House, 15 Dawson Place, London W2 4TH, tel. 01 221 5538 is owned and run by Richard and Jenny Freeman. Their 80 page catalogue is a work of art and a mine of information about the superlative champagnes they import (and the grower-owners and their families). In addition to the well known favourites Bollinger, Moet & Chandon, Perrier-Jouet, Mumm, Pol Roger and Ruinart there are a dozen or so smaller suppliers each with a special quality. For instance, Albert le Brun of Avize and Chalons sur Marne; Robert Billion of Le Mesnil sur Oger; R. Driant and Roland Fliniaux of Ay; Paul Goerg of Vertus; R. & L. Legras of Chouilly; A. Seconde Prevoteau of Ambonnay. Try the Champagne House tasting case @ £150. Twelve bottles, seven styles and ten different shippers.

(b) Champagne de Villages, Park House, 29 Fonnereau

73

Road, Ipswich, Suffolk, tel. 0473 56922 is run by Tony Westbrook. He has discovered another range of small vignerons who produce good value champagnes. Jean Paul Arvois of Charot, Michel Labbé of Chamery, Pierre Arnould of Verzenay, Gilbert Bertrand of Chamery, Raymond Devilliers of Villedommange, Georges Lilbert of Cramant, Jacques Copinet of Montgenost and Alexandre Bonnet of Les Riceys. Also imported are a range of Côteaux Champenois still wines, Rosé de Riceys, Ratafia and Marc de Champagne. Altogether a very intriguing selection.

(c)   Now Lay and Wheeler was *the* Wine Merchant of the Year for 1988 (a Sunday Telegraph and Wine Magazine award) and it is interesting to see what they have to offer in their champagne range. They have 16 non-vintage wines, six vintage and nine up-market luxury Cuvées with prices nearly up to £100 per bottle for 1961 Krug Collection. Their own brand is described as 'fragrant, delicate, beautifully clean, and scintillatingly fresh'. Shipper's wines include Ellner, Mercier, Laurent, Perrier, Lanson, Moet et Chandon, Joseph Perrier, Veuve Clicquot, Taittinger, Bollinger and Krug. They, particularly like the Louis Roederer range, of which 75% is produced from their own vineyards.

Further information

For 'amateurs de vin de champagne' apart from reading the bibliography at the end of this book, I have some advice.

(1)   Buy some champagne from these specialist importers having read their catalogue carefully.

(2)   Attend a champagne appreciation course — Grants of St. James School of Wine, Guildford Cellars, Moorfield Road, Guildford, Surrey GU1 1RU. They run courses twice a year, usually in June and September of four days, priced at £460 to include transport, more-than-adequate accommodation, meals with wine, talks, tastings and visits.

(3)   A full list of courses and tours is available from Wine Development Board, 5 Kings House, Kennet Wharf Lane, Upper Thames Street, London EC4V 3BH.

(4)   Some independent wine merchants such as La Vigneronne, 105 Old Brompton Road, London SW7 3LE have tutored champagne tastings often at the nearby Bailey's Hotel. Recently a blind tasting of 1979 vintage champagnes would have cost you £18.50 a ticket. However, you could have tasted and retasted Veuve Clicquot, Bollinger, Renaudin, Roederer Crystal and Perrier Jouet Belle Epoque — a selection of nine superb vintage wines.

Points for style

What is style? Set twelve Masters of Wine into one tasting room, give them one champagne to taste — blind, i.e. without knowing its provenance — and you will get very mixed opinions. Do not be discouraged, however, it is your individual palate that matters. If you like your Champers 'doux' or bone-dry that is your affair and the experts' opinion need not concern you. Nevertheless, the following notes may be of help. They are produced from a wide variety of sources.

Bricout — straw colour, full creamy nose, soft ripe fruit, subtle biscuity overtones, clean finish, good mousse.

Jacquart champagne — elegant, creamy, refreshing with light, perfectly balanced fruitiness.

Louis Roederer Blanc de Blancs — immense finesse, subtle and long in flavour, very pale peach in colouring.

Krug Rosé Brut — pale copper, sparse beading to look at. Nose of rich baked bread, peach and almond. Taste dry, full bodied, intense, rich, toasty, walnut, green apple, well integrated, complex long, elegant, full fruity finish.

Bollinger Special Cuvée — a superb rich, biscuity powerful champagne.

De Venoge Cordon Bleu — soft, a little bit sweet, needing a little more acidity, but mature with biscuity fruit of well-aged champagne.

75

CHAMPAGNE ON A BUDGET

J. de Telmont Grande Reserve Brût — pale gold, delicious, big rich biscuity mouthful, a black grape dominated wine. Also lively, fruity flavour, good yeasty character.

Champagne Lambert Grande Reserve — fresh, properly dry and acid, mature with slight tartness.

Pol Roger NV — consistently good full flavoured classic, firm flavour, good lingering balance.

Sainsbury's Blanc de Blanc Vintage (from Linard Gontier) — refined, toasted almond scent, rich and mature and toasty palate.

Michel Labbé (Champagne de Villages) Brut — predominantly Pinot Noir, with a little Pinot Meunier. Extremely fine and elegant champagne with a creamy mousse, crisp fragrant nose, soft on the palate.

Robert Billion (Champagne House) — wonderfully fragrant, flowery, long lasting wine, immensely powerful, remarkable gout de terroir.

Moet et Chandon NV Brut — warm fruity taste, firm backbone of colour with rich golden tone.

Mumm Cordon Rouge NV — agreeable fresh, young, green, yeasty champagne but with a short finish.

Perrier-Jouet Brut 1979 — defined complexion, rich and flavourful. In colour pale greenish-gold, steady beading with tight bubbles. Nose — butter, toast and smoke. Taste — dry, full bodied, crisp, clean, rich toasty and buttery, very well balanced with good acidity.

Veuve Clicquot Rosé Brut Vintage — deep burnt orange-salmon, good steady beading. Nose — baked bread, toasty, orange peel. Taste — dry, full bodied, baked bread, good acid and balance, hard nutty finish that stays with you!

Champagne Vintages

Usually individual champagne houses 'declared', as do the port wine shippers, a single wine of a specific year after they found the quality of the young wine to be exceptional. It was then held for up to six or seven years in their cellars before being released at a premium price to the wealthy cognoscenti. Recently a few shippers have cashed in on the profit potential by declaring a vintage *every* year irrespective of the intrinsic wine quality and then compounding their *crime* by harbouring the wine for only four or five years before putting it on the market. So here's my handy guide to help you pick the best wines produced over the last nine years.

1987:An average year with more rain than usual, probably ought not to have been declared.

1986:As above.

1985:Probably going to be an excellent vintage year, but a small crop.

1984:Definitely should not be classified as a vintage year.

1983:Almost certainly now an excellent vintage wine. Large crop.

1982:Best vintage year for a long time. Large crop.

1981:Very small crop, not declared as vintage but good quality.

1980:Very small crop, indifferent quality.

1979:Excellent vintage, declared by most shippers.

You can find vintage champagnes at the stockists listed below:
— Majestic Wine offer two 1979's, one 1981 and three 1982 vintages (including one rosé).

— Lay and Wheeler offer 1979, 1980, 1981 and 1982· vintages.

— The Champagne House offer 1979, 1980 and 1982 vintage wines.

— Champagne de Villages offer a 1981 and 1982.

— Some of the best vintage wine shippers are Louis Roederer, Pol Roger, Veuve Clicquot and Joseph Perrier.

CHAPTER NINE:
A FEAST FOR THE TASTE BUDS

Covering a wide and varied region of three different departements it seems logical to approach this delicious subject as though one was being treated to a long and sumptuous meal.

Starters

For hors d'oeuvre-entrees, the jambon de Reims is well known, particularly jambon en croute (ham cooked in pastry). Now the French over the centuries have brought to an art, the wide and varied end products from the domestic pig or 'cochon'. Andouille is a red/black large pork, tripe and chitterling sausage, sliced thinly and served cold, whereas Andouillette is a smaller but similar version served hot. These come from Troyes and many parts of the Aube. Troyes produces a wide range of pork sausages and pork brawn. Tripes à la tomate come from Chateauvillan (Haute Marne). Terrines and patés wrapped in pastry feature around Reims. Again from Troyes come stuffed pig's tongue, truffled pig's feet and smoked lamb's tongue.

The French invented paté. The Champagne area produced a wide range, of anguille (eel), bécasse (woodcock), canard (duck), lapin (rabbit), grives (poor little thrushes), sometimes in a pastry. Paté de pigeons en croute is a speciality from Reims and paté champenois aux morrilles d'Essoyes comes from the Aube. Try Boudin blanc, i.e. not a black pudding that we might find in our north country but a whiter version filled with all sorts of pig's bits and pieces. Pig's trotters, either cold as an hors d'oeuvre, or as a main course served hot, would have come as 'pieds de cochon' from Sainte Ménéhould (Marne).

The trotters are cooked slowly for several hours until the bones etc. are soft!

Troyes (Aube) also produces an unusual entrée — langue de mouton fumée i.e. smoked sheep's tongue. Snails (escargots) are a unique French speciality usually spiced with garlic and served hot or cold. Escargots de Champagne are almost as well known as their neighbours escargots de Bourgogne. Choucroute is a form of cabbage similar to the German sauerkraut and this often forms part of the cold crudités. Brienne le Chateau (Aube) produces this dish.

Fish dishes

A fish course next. Champagne has a dozen rivers and another dozen large freshwater lakes. Trout from Bar, Estissac and Laignes (Aube), truite à la creme from the Haute Marne. The rivers la Laignes, la Vanne, produce trout and pike (sometimes cooked in champagne). Look out too for cervelat de poisson from the Marne and salmon from the river Vanne (Aube). Ecrevisses (freshwater crayfish) are often on the menu. So too are quennelles and soufflés of pike, or better still pike braised in champagne. Eel is encountered as part of 'fritures' (a fry up) and matelotes (fish stews). 'Anguille au vert' is eel cooked in a green herb wine sauce.

Meat specialities

For the meat course, game pie with venison or wild boar is a great delicacy and served as 'gigue (haunch) de sanglier'. Roe deer (chevreuil) from the many forests is also an unusual treat. Beef (boeuf) is a speciality from Bassigny (Haute Marne). Côte de porc comes from all over Champagne — a good staple dish. Cachuse or caqhuse is a pork dish braised with onions. A popular local meat dish is potée des vendangeurs (vintagers) or potée Champenoise — a splendid thick country stew of sausage, smoked ham, bacon with cabbage and other vegetables — simmered for some time and served piping hot. Another staple is coq au vin, coq à la biere, or better still poulet au Champagne. An unusual dish is 'pied de mouton farcis' i.e. sheep's feet stuffed with garlic. Kidneys are popular especially 'rognons au champagne' (Marne). From Estissac (Aube) come meat croquettes and pavés with minced pork, herbs and vegetables. Rabbit (lapin) is often on the menu stewed or braised.

Vegetable course

Vegetables are usually served as a separate course. Asparagus from Hermonville (Marne), choux (cabbage) from Ecury (Marne), champignons (mushroons) de prairie et de forêt. Flamiche de l'Aube is leek or pumpkin and cream tart.

Your salad may well be salade au lard (bacon). Gougères des Riceys is a speciality from the Aube — a hot pastry filled with cauliflower cheese. Salade de pissenlits au lard sounds rather vulgar but is delicious — dandelion leaves with diced bacon, fried bread or possibly potatoes.

Cheese choice

The cheese board anywhere in France is tempting. Nowhere more so than in Champagne. Troyes once again specialises in cheeses from nearby Chaource, Eclance, Ervy le Chatel and Mussy and goat cheeses from the Pays d'Othe. Other goat cheeses, sharp and pungent come from villages in the Marne. 'Caprice des Dieux' (a commercial mild, soft double cream cheese, in oval shapes with a white rind) from Langres and Bourmont (Haute Marne). The Marne produces 'fromage cendre' (also from les Riceys, Aube), a soft skimmed milk cheese, coated with ashes giving a nutty flavour.

Fromage de Langres (Haute Marne) is tangy with a pungent smell and brown red rind. From Igny Complizy (Marne) the Trappist monks produce a large mild cheese with yellow rind from their monastery. An Emmenthal style cheese is made at Illoud, Pieremont sur Amance, and Balesmes villages in the Haute Marne. Chaumont (Haute Marne) produces a spicy, strong smelling cheese, and Arrigny (Marne) also produces a good local cheese. From Rolamport (Haute Marne) comes Tarte au Fromage Blanc le Guémeu, served hot or cold. The

best season for cheeses if you like them young and fresh is
May — October.

Super sweets

Fruit is plentiful either fresh — cerises (cherries) de Dormans
(Aube) or fraises (strawberries) de Merfy (Marne) — or as
Anglois (plum tart), rabote (white apple in a pastry case, not a
soggy dumpling). Caisses de Bar is a meringue with almonds
from the Aube. Crêpes à la myrtille are bilberry pancakes from
Mandres la Côte (Haute Marne).

   Sweet toothed travellers can try Bouchons de Champagne,
pain d'épices (spiced honey gingerbread), biscuit de Reims
(small oblong macaroons) and chocomailles (chocolate figures
from the Aube). Rondeau de Champagne and Massepain are
other sweet dishes from Reims (Marne). Champardennois
gateaux (rich cakes), meringues from Wassy (Haute Marne),
croquignoles (a crunchy sweet biscuit) and pink Reims biscuits
are favourites in the Marne.

Guided tours

Incidentally, many food speciality firms are open to visitors
for guided tours and I have chosen a mixed dozen.

●**Aube** (telephone code 25)
   — Champignonière de Paris, 10300 Montgueux, tel.
74 84 79. M. Henry Papillon will show you, not butterflies,
but the culture and production of mushrooms.

   — Elevage de chevres de Maraye, rue Haute, 10160 Maraye
en Othe, tel. 70 11 61. M. Brouillet will show you goat
cheeses being made, with tastings!

   — Pisciculture de la Vanne, Moulin d'Estissac, 10190
Estissac, tel. 40 42 18. M. Mesley will show in an 18th
century windmill his trout and salmon hatchery.

   — Two more fromageries are Thomas & Desplats, 10210
Blanot la Grange, tel. 70 02 98 and Pierre Henry, 10130
Courson en Othe, tel. 42 12 14.

— Another fishy place is Patrick Bachelier, 10700 Trolans, tel. 37 31 15, who has an llth century 'moulin champenois' for his trout farm and hatchery.

— Fromagerie Hugerot, 10210 Maisons les Chaource, tel. 40 16 33, makes the well known delicate fruity Chaource cheese.

— Le Bon Pain de France, 9 rue Raymond Poincare, 10300 Ste. Savine, makes bread, gateaux (cakes) and your breakfast croissants.

— Etablissement Bellot, 10210 Chaource, tel. 40 11 01 is a cider making firm.

— Etablissement Laurent, Blignicourt, 10500 Brienne le Chateau, tel. 92 16 06, makes choucrouterie (sauerkraut) on a commercial scale.

— Fromagerie d'Eclance, 10200 Eclance, tel. 26 40 03. M. Turin will show you his cheese specialities being made.

— Co-operateurs de Champagne, 114, Boulevard de Dijon, 10800 St Julien les Villas, tel. 82 32 12 are a commercial charcuterie-boucherie firm — perhaps not for the faint hearted!

●**Haute Marne** (telephone code 25)

— Two fromageries are Schertenleib, 52140 Saulxures, tel. 86 13 20) who make fromage de Langres; and Emmenthal style at Societé Elnor, Route de Montigny, 52200 Langres, tel. 87 44 92.

What to drink

To end your Champagne country meal, try the Marc de Champagne (a type of brandy), Fine de Marne, Prunelles de Champagne from Arcis and Troyes (sloe gin), Noisette and Mirabelle de Lorraine in the Haute Marne. Incidentally, I have assumed that you started your meal with a coupe de champagne. An alternative is Ratafia, a mixture of still sweet white wine of Champagne and of Marc. Watch your host carefully to make sure he gets the proportions right.

You can wash each 'plat' down with champagne. Amongst the alternatives are Vin Rosé from Les Riceys (Aube), honest vin de table from Montgueux (near Troyes), from Coiffy (Haute Marne), the well-named Le Bouzy famed from the 17th century with its bouquet and 'goût de pêche' (taste of peach). The Coteaux Champenois wines come from the Marne and the Aube, from many villages including a red from Balnot (Aube). There are dozens of small villages in the southern Marne and the Aube producing excellent white, red and occasional AOC Coteaux Champenois still table wines.

Sample menus

To end this chapter I have chosen a dozen mouth watering dishes from restaurants all over Champagne country. In all probability they will *not* be included in the modest prix fixé menus but they show you what's available when the purse strings are loosened. There are four from each departement.

●**Aube** (tel. code 25)

— *Brevonnes* 10220 Piney — Le Vieux Logis, tel. 46 30 17. Mignardise de volaille champenoise; Filet de lotte (burbot eel) braisé au vin des Riceys.

— *Nogent sur Seine* 10400 — Le Beau Rivage, tel. 39 84 22. Truitte de la Vanne en crepinettes.

— *Troyes* 10000 — Au Chateaubriand, 31 rue Voltaire, tel. 79 20 04
Cuisse de lapin aux noisettes Foret d'Othe; Blanquette de Saint Jacques au champagne.

— *Mailly le Camp* 10230 — Le Saint Eloi, 4 rue de Chalons, tel. 37 30 04.
Truite aux amandes; lapin à la moutarde.

●**Marne** (tel. code 26)

— *Ambonnay* 51150 — Auberge St. Vincent, 1 rue St. Vincent, tel. 57 01 98.
Boudin (meat pudding) de lapin champenoise; Matelotte d'anquille (eel) à l'Ambonnay.

— *Beaumont sur Vesle* 51400 — La Maison du Champagne, 2 rue du Port, tel. 03 92 45.
Tripes au champagne; rognons de veau au ratafia.

— *Dormans* 51700 — La Table Sourdet, 5 rue du Dr. Moret, tel. 58 20 57.
Brochet de Marne au beurre blanc; Coq au vin rouge de champagne.

— *Sainte Mènèhould* 51800 — Le Cheval Rouge, 1–3 rue Chanzy, tel. 60 81 04.
Pied de cochon à la Sainte Mènèhould; tarte soufflée aux fruits rouges.

●**Haute Marne** (tel. code 25)

— *Langres* 52200 — Le Diderot, 4 rue de l'Estres, tel. 87 07 00.
Feuillete d'escargots (snails); Escalope saumon rosé à la fleur de moutarde.

— *Montigny le Roi* 52140 — InterHotel Moderne, Avenue Lierneux, tel. 90 30 18.
Salade gourmande; Escalope de boeuf aux cèpes (cep mushrooms).

— *St. Dizier* 52100 — Le Relais des Nations, Route Vitry, tel. 05 07 97.
Assiette du pecheur; Cassolette d'escargots aux cèpes.

— *Perthes* 52100 — Relais Paris-Strasbourg, 6 Route National, tel. 55 40 64.
Supreme de volaille farci, 'Café de Paris'; magret de canard aux pommes.

CHAPTER TEN:
THE MARNE — NOTABLE
TOWNS AND VILLAGES

The Marne is shaped like a large butterfly, with a land mass of nearly 5,000 sq. km. and a population of 550,000. To the north is the departement of the Ardennes, to the east the Meuse, to the south the Aube and Haute Marne and to the west the Aisne. The Marne, of course, is the major river bisecting the departement with Epernay, Chalons sur Marne and Vitry le Francois bordering it. Reims is on the River Vesle, Sezanne in the south west is near the Grand Morin and Sainte Ménéhould in the east on the River Aisne. The autoroute charges through the Marne from Paris through the southern suburbs of Reims and east towards the south of Sainte Ménéhould in the direction of Metz. The huge man-made lake and reservoir of Der-Chantecoq is in the deep south east of the departement bordering the Haute Marne.

The Marne has many facets to show the traveller. There are nearly a hundred small villages off the beaten track, each with a little romanesque church dating from the 11th or 12th century. It is the centre of the great champagne industry with 60 wine villages clustering around Reims and Epernay. It has a score of rather sad mementos of World War I — battlefields, cemeteries and war museums. The grand cathedrals and abbeys at Reims, Chalons and l'Epine are outstanding examples of the gothic champenoise style of architecture.

Of course, besides drinking your flute of champagne on frequent occasions, you will find that the locals not only feed themselves remarkably well but have dozens of delightful little restaurants to tempt you too.

Bonne route!

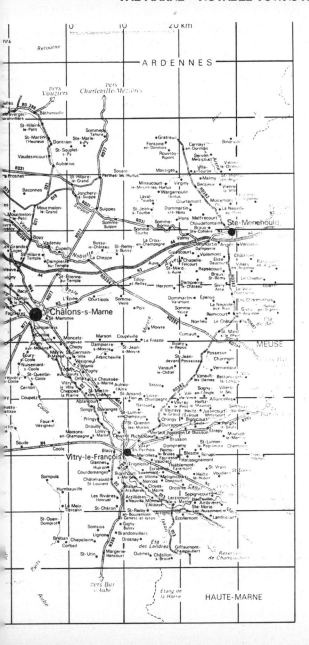

Reims

The Ville Sainte (the sacred city) of France, Reims (or Rheims), population 180,000, has a documented history of over 2,000 years. Their medieval archbishops created immense prestige and of course wealth, deriving in the main from the great trade fairs. As a result no less than 25 kings of France have been crowned in the great cathedral of Notre Dame. Clovis was the first and Charles X was the last to be crowned. It is appropriate that Reims has been twinned since 1962 with our holy city of Canterbury. Nobody looking at Reims today can possibly envisage the damage done by the original Vandals and more recently by the modern vandals of the north in World War I. The resilience of the modern 'Rémois' cannot be overstated. Although the city is not on a main river (rare in France) it lies at the centre of the ancient trade routes and more recently its huge chalk cellars have been holding more and more liquid gold wealth. These cellars deep in the chalk were first dug by the Roman slaves. They were originally chalk pits and the excavated chalk was used to build the Roman town houses and villas. During the savage bombardment of World War I most of the population took refuge deep down in the chalk cellars. In the next war the cellars of Moet et Chandon and Piper Heidsieck were used by the Resistance to store firearms and explosives. One could hide anything in the 100 km. of chalk galleries!

Reims was evangelised in the 3rd century during the 'Pax Romana' and the city was so dignified and elegant that it was called 'the second Rome', being the seat of the Roman Governor of the province of Belgium. Sainte Sixte created the first bishopric at the end of the 3rd century and during the 8th century it became an archbishopric.

After the Romans left, the power vacuum was filled by the Vandals who promptly martyred the Bishop Nicaise outside his church in AD 407. Fortunately the next invaders, the Franks, were less ferocious and Bishop Remi baptised Clovis the pagan King of the Franks in AD 498 in the Cathedral of Saint Nicaise. Charlemagne in the 9th century regarded the city with favour and prosperity continued until a major fire in AD 1210 destroyed the cathedral and most of the town. In

1359 King Edward III tried to get himself crowned at Reims — but was refused.

The people of Champagne and indeed most of France, took heart when Charles VII was crowned on 17th July 1479 in the presence of Joan of Arc. The English armies had ravaged the north of France (Crécy and Agincourt) and the Maid of Orleans gave the French the courage they desperately needed.

The university was built in 1547 and the city has been a centre of the arts ever since. The wine trade prosperity, largely created by Dom Perignon's discovery, brought even more wealth to the region until the gallant new 'citoyens' of the Revolution at the end of the 18th century destroyed it. The grand abbeys of St. Denis, les Cordeliers and St. Nicaise were partly destroyed in the mass hysteria.

After World War I, the rubble of 12,000 houses was cleared away and wide, dignified, straight boulevards were built — similar to those in Paris. So Reims now is a large prosperous city of 180,000 people, well laid out and with many attractions.

The great buildings, the cathedral of Notre Dame, the Palais du Tau, the Basilique St. Remi and the various museums are covered in the next chapter. So too are the champagne houses (Pommery, Taittinger, Veuve Clicquot, Mumm etc.) clustered around the Champ de Mars and the parklands covering the rocky 'crayères'.

The site of the Roman Porte de Mars should be visited. Legend has it that the Roman Emperor Probus authorised the resumption of vine cultivation. Two centuries earlier, to protect the home industry, another Roman Emperor had decreed that all Gallic vines should be dug up! The grateful citizens then at their own cost erected the enormous Porte de Mars to thank Probus, not for any military exploits but for returning their wine trade prosperity to them.

The main shopping centres, including the Marks & Spencer store, are within easy walking distance west of the cathedral. Along the boulevards there are many restaurants, cafés, brasseries and in the rue Talleyrand, two mouthwatering chocolate shops opposite each other — Fonie Chocquelaterie and Jeff de Bruges. You will have endless opportunities to taste champagne. Most brasseries and wine bars charge 20 francs or so for a good 'coupe de champagne'.

A two day visit to Reims could take in a champagne house visit one morning and in the afternoon the Basilique St. Remi and its museum of the same name. The following day a visit to the cathedral of Notre Dame, its Treasury (Palais du Tau) in the Place Royale and perhaps the Vintage Car Museum. Then after lunch a look at the Porte de Mars and a visit to a different champagne house. If it is fine, sit in the sun in the Parc Pommery and plan which restaurant you are going to visit (see Chapter Twelve).

For hotels try the Porte Paris, the Chateaubriand or the Hotel Linquet. There are three modest hotels in the rue Thillois, a road off the south side of the main Place Drouet d'Erlon. For a good meal try La Boule d'Or, 39 rue Thiers, which bisects the rue Talleyrand opposite the station. For free parking look along the length of the wide boulevards in front of the station in Boulevard Louis Roederer.

Local tours

Reims has a western local tour circuit of interest mainly through wine villages. Take the N31 west towards Soissons across the Canal de l'Aisne and the River Vesle (Michelin Map 56). About 6 km. out, turn right on the D26 to Chalons sur Vesle, then to Chenay, west to Trigny (Cave Co-operative), north to Hermonville (11th century church) which the English unfortunately destroyed in 1373. West to Bouvancourt on the D30 (19th century chateau de Vaux Varennes), Ventelay, Romain. South west to Courlandon, to Fismes (population 4,300) a former textile centre where Napoleon stayed in 1814 in hot pursuit of Blucher. The village was destroyed by the Germans in 1918. Next south to St. Gilles (a beautiful romanesque church with octagonal tower), Courville (following the River Ardre), with another fine romanesque church with a saddleback roof tower, on the D386 to Crugny (an 11th century church), across the river to Arcis le Ponsart. The abbey of Igny 3 km. south in a wooded ravine, was founded in 1126 by the monks of Clairvaux and is occupied now by Trappist monks of Laval. The ruined chateau, 12th century church and the local artisans (pottery and tanned skin products) are worth a stop.

Lagery, south east on the D25 and D27 has a medieval chateau and a church of note. L'Hery (12th century church), over the autoroute, then the D380 to Romigny (romanesque church), east to Ville en Tardenois, badly damaged in World War I, but with a well repaired church, Chambrecy, Chaumuzy which has a monument to the Italian soldiers killed in 1914-18, and more mundanely, a wine Cave Co-operative. South east to Marfaux, with a squat romanesque church and a vigneron co-operative, on the D386 and just outside is a British war cemetery (sadly there are others nearby at Courmas, Bouilly and Chambrecy). Pourcy has the Maison du Parc Regional at the entrance to the Forest, Nanteuil la Foret across the River Ardre to Saint Imoges. Legend has it that a statue of Virgin la Sainte Image was discovered in the heart of an oaktree in the 18th century. The village church has a unique bell carillon. The annual pilgrimage to Notre Dame du Chêne takes place on the second Sunday in September. A joint French/British cemetery is near the main road N51. The Maison du Vigneron de Champagne here has tasting facilities and a restaurant.

Keep east on the D71 to Germaine (see the Musée du Bucheron — the cork museum). East north east to Ville en Selve on the D71, Craon de Ludes and Ludes where St. Vincent de Paul preached in 1645. A vigneron Co-operative, Canard Duchêne (the duck in the oak tree) and Ployez Jacquemart are here and just to the east is Mailly Champagne which has an important Cave Co-operative.

Verzenay and Verzy are two top class champagne villages just to the east of Mailly Champagne. The former has a notable windmill, a Cave Co-operative and wine producer Emile Michel (tel. 26 49 40 40) and Eugene Ralle (tel. 26 49 40 12) and the latter has Sacy, 6 rue de Verzenay (tel. 26 97 91 13). Verzy is a town with historical background. Two saints, Basle (575) and Nivart (664) lived here and built a monastery. Before contemplating an attack on Reims, our King Edward III used Verzy as his army headquarters. The nearby observatory

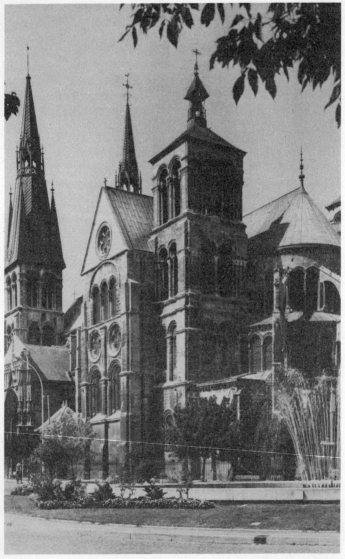

Chalon Sur Marne – église

called Mount Sinai was the French headquarters where General Gouraud prepared the final French offensives in 1918. Both villages (population 1,250) are worth a visit.

To the west of Mailly and Ludes on the D26 is another well known wine village, Rilly la Montagne (population 1,200) with a large co-operative, H. Germain & Fils, 38 rue de Reims (tel. 26 03 40 19) and Gardet in the commune at Chigny les Roses (tel. 26 03 42 03). Villers Allerand nestles under Mont Joli and has a romanesque church. Back to Reims via Champfleury where the Allied troops who finally defeated Napoleon camped in spring of 1814. Finally 10 km. into the southern suburbs of Reims (Murigny, la Maison Blanche).

Chalons sur Marne

This town with a population of 55,000 is 45 km. drive south east of Reims by the N44, an easy and pleasant drive. Look at the Fort de la Pompelle 9 km. out of Reims, which has a military museum and war time trenches — a famous French battle 'monument'.

Chalons was an important Roman city under Emperor Augustus and was the Legion headquarters of the north east. It was evangelised in the 3rd century by Saint Memmie. In AD 451 several battles took place in the area between Chalons and Troyes during which Attila the Hun was eventually beaten after immense slaughter on both sides. The Allied army was commanded by the Roman General Aetius and the Visigoth King Theodore was killed in the bloody fight which saved Christendon.

In Chalons, St. Bernard preached the second Crusade in AD 1147. For several centuries the bishopric of Chalons was so important that the region was independent of the Royal House (Henri III called it the Principal Town in Champagne) almost until the Revolution. Marie Antoinette visited Chalons several times in the period 1770–1791. Chalons then became the Prefecture town under the Napoleonic Consulat era and became a major army garrison in 1856. During World War I the Germans bombarded the town in 1914 and 1918 and damaged it even more seriously during World War II in 1940.

Despite these ravages, Chalons has preserved three outstanding buildings, the 13th century cathedral of St. Etienne, the church and cloisters of Notre Dame en Vaux. The centre is most attractive, the River Marne and several canals meander through the town. There are many public gardens including the Jardin Anglais beside the Marne. The Syndicat d'Initiative guided tour is very good value. Their office is in the Place Godart near the Hotel de Ville.

There are two champagne houses in Chalons; Albert le Brun, 93 Avenue de Paris (tel. 26 68 18 68); Joseph Perrier, 69 Avenue de Paris (tel. 26 68 29 51). They are on the west bank quite close to the SNCF Gare. For modest hotels try the Jolly, the Moritz or le Chemin de Fer and for restaurants, l'Avenue, 82 Avenue de Sainte Ménéhould with menu from 40 francs. Their specialities are viandes grillées sur adoise and diablotins d'escargots.

Suggestions for visits around Chalons are as follows, both along the Marne either north west or south east. The former starts with the D1 via Juvigny, Vraux, Aigny, Tours sur Marne (see A. Chauvet, 11 Avenue de Champagne and Veuve Laurent Perrier, also in the same street). South across the river to Athis (chateau) and back to Chalons via Jalons (romanesque church and crypt), Aulnay sur Marne, Matouges, St. Gibrien (which takes its name from an Irish hermit who retired here in the 7th century) and Fagnières.

The south east tour starts on the N44 at St. Memmie (population 7,000), a suburb of Chalons which takes its name from the first bishop buried here in the 4th century. A small abbey, now a retirement home, can still be seen. Chepy, St. Germain la Ville, Pogny (with a 12th century church which has a notable nave). By contrast the world's largest silo, holding 110,000 tons of lucerne is here! Omey, la Chaussée sur Marne (the church of St. Pierre de Coulmiers built in the 12th century is notable), then cross over the river to St. Martin aux Champs and back towards Chalons on the D2. Cleppes la Prairie, Vitry la Ville (chateau), Togny aux Boeufs and Mairy sur Marne. Here our Jacobite King James of Scotland stayed in the chateau during much of his exile. Keep on the D2, the airport of Ecury sur Code is 2 km. to the west and via Coolus and

Compertrix back into Chalons.

To the north east of Chalons via the D77 and D394 near the River Noblette is la Cheppe, a prehistoric fortified camp of the latter iron age. This site is called Camp d'Attila where the horrible Hun fought one of his battles. A small temple to Minerva 'Forum Minervae' can be seen. Also to the north east 6 km. on the N3 signed for Sainte Ménéhould is the church of Notre Dame at l'Epine, an important pilgrimage site from the 13th century — and still is, between March — October. The huge basilique is a treasure of late Gothic style. An awe-inspiring sight rising above the Champagne plain. There are important music festivals in June.

Epernay

This town with a population of 30,000, is equidistant from Reims or Chalons. Looking at this placid, prosperous Champagne town it is hard to believe that it has suffered even more in the past than most French towns. The English armies were here during the Hundred Years War. In 1432 the inhabitants were banned 'proscrits' from their town for three years! King Francis I ordered the town to be burnt in 1544. King Henry IV besieged it during the wars of religion in 1592, when he was still a Huguenot. Plague has wiped out its population, famine has killed them off, the River Marne has overflowed its banks and inundated the town! The Bavarian army occupied it in 1814–15 and the Prussians in 1870–71. It was rebuilt after the 1914–18 bombardments and was occupied 1940–44 by the Wehrmacht until liberation by General Patton.

One reason why it has always attracted so many marauding armies has undoubtedly been the lure of its liquid gold! It has some noteworthy buildings (see Chapter Eleven) and museums. A determined visit down the Avenue de Champagnes will keep you busy for days. The shippers who give tours without needing prior notice are the sophisticated Moet & Chandon, de Castellane (57 rue de Verdun), Mercier and de Venoge; but the other 30 will be pleased to do so by written or telephone appointment. A local firm, Decouverte, tel. 26 54 19 49, will take you on minibus tours on the three wine circuits and collect and deliver you back to your hotel (English spoken). Paul Gobillard, Chateau de Pierry, tel. 26 54 05 11, offer the visitor a day's visit, tasting, tour, a magnificent lunch and a champagne tea with patisserie. Wine groups are preferred and a recent cost was 250 francs per person.

On 22nd January, St. Vincent's Day is celebrated with processions and feastings in Ambonnay, Ay, Chamery, Champillon, Damery, Hautvillers, Verzenay and Verzy by the various local Committees and Confreries.

The wine museum at 13 Avenue de Champagne is worth a visit (7 francs). There are several good value hotels including la Terrasse, St. Pierre, du Progres and le Palais. Also Le Chapon Fin, du Soleil and the Pub Stella. There are also modest hotels at Montmort Lucy, Vertus, Tours sur Marne, Germaine, Baye, St. Imoges and Vauciennes. For restaurants, my preference is for La Terrasse, Chez l'Hermine and Chez Max. Epernay is twinned with Clevedon in the UK, mainly because of their rugby team's activities. Regional wine tours are covered in Chapter Seven.

Vitry le Francois

Vitry is the capital of the Perthois region and is 32 km. south east on the N44 from Chalons. It has a population of 20,000 — see Michelin Map 61. It is a large industrial town on the River Marne and two canals. The modern architecture reflects the fact that two German bombardments in 1940 destroyed 90% of the town. It is a miracle that any pre-1944 buildings exist (see Chapter Eleven). The hotel le Bon Séjour, 2–4 Faubourg Léon Bourgeois and the restaurant Le Gourmet des Halles, 11 rue des Soeurs are both good value.

To the south east of Vitry is St. Dizier in the Haute Marne, 29 km. on the N4 (see Chapter Twelve). Also south east on the D13 approximately 15 km. is the huge Lac du Der Chantecoq (see Chapter Twenty-Two). The whole area is heavily wooded with rivers, streams, canals and lakes.

There are many charming small villages quite unspoilt by modern 'progress' such as Chatillon sur Broue, Drosnay, Outines, St. Amand sur Fion, Sainte Marie du Lac and

Sermaize les Bains (population 2,600) on the N395. Here there is a Roman site, on which a Benedictine Abbey was built, subsequently visited by Kings Francis I, Charles IX and Louis XIV. Mineral and spa waters were discovered and the 'fountain of the Saracens' is the name given to the water source. The town was the limit of the German advance in 1914. A romanesque 12th century church and a huge sugar and spirit distillery are in the town.

Sainte Ménéhould

In the north east corner of the departement (Map 56) equidistant from Vitry le Francois (D382) and Chalons sur Marne (N3) is Sainte Ménéhould (population 6,000). The autoroute A4 passes just to the south of the town which is classified as a 'Station Verte de Vacances' (countryside holiday resort). Once the town was fortified by its own ramparts. A terrible fire in 1719 destroyed the old town completely except for a 13th century brick church called the Chateau Church on the hill overlooking the town. After the great fire an ancestor of mine — one of the King's architects — Philippe de la Force, reconstructed the city. Please do not blame me if you disagree with his choice of rose coloured bricks, etc.

On 21st June 1791 the local postmaster called J. B. Drouet, recognised the wretched King Louis XVI fleeing from Paris to Metz and arranged for his monarch's arrest at Varennes. What a worthy 'citoyen'! The champagne monk Dom Perignon was born and bred here although he made his vinous discoveries in Hautvillers.

Pig's trotters are the gourmet speciality of Sainte Ménéhould. Try the Hotel de la Poste which has a decent restaurant or Le Cheval Rouge where you can have 'Pied de Cochon à la Sainte Ménéhould'!

The east side of the town is heavily wooded and the forests of the Argonne start here. To the west 6 km. on the N3 is the Chateau de Braux Sainte Cohière, which has a mid-summer festival of Valmy, where in 1792 the 'Sans Culottes', the derisory phrase for the young revolutionary soldiers, managed to send the Prussians packing. The hill overlooking the

97

battlefield is called Mont Kellermann after the French general in command. The casualties were few in that engagement but the many cemeteries in the Argonne area show where the French and their Allies fought and died in World War I.

Sézanne

In the south west corner of the departement is Sézanne (population 6,200 — Map 61) which is 44 km. from Epernay (D51) to the north and 57 km. from Chalons sur Marne (N4) to the east. A priory was built here in AD 1085 by the monks of Cluny and ramparts, wells, narrow streets give provincial charm to the town. The 16th century church of St. Denis is notable, as is the 'Mail des Cordeliers', a chestnut tree lined road along the ramparts towards the chateau which still has two intact towers. The food speciality is andouillettes (sliced pork meats).

Sézanne has some champagne growing vineyards — see Granier in the town. Duval Leroy own vineyards locally and the wine Côte de Sézanne extends from 15 km. north east of the town in a narrow band 35 km. south and south west of the town, including Barbonne Fayel, Saudoy, Vindey and Bethon. The local still wine is drinkable. Try the hotel-restaurant La Croix d'Or or the Relais Champenois et du Lion d'Or. The restaurant Le Soleil has a good reputation too.

Some other curiosities in the Marne

— *Brimont:* north of Reims was occupied by the English army in 1359 and in 1914–18 by the German army.

— *Brugny Vaudancourt*: south west of Epernay, was destroyed by the English in the Hundred Years War.

— *Bussy le Chateau*: north east of Chalons, was another of Attila the Hun's battlefields.

— *Chambrecy*: south west of Reims, has a World War I cemetery of English and Italian dead.

— *Champaubert*: halfway between Epernay and Sézanne, was a battlefield where on 10th February 1814 Napoleon beat the Russian army.

— *Chaudefontaine*: 2 km. north of Sainte Ménéhould, as its name implies has an 11th century river, source of the 'Calida Fontana' which has *never* been known to freeze over.

— *Conflans sur Seine*: south west of Sèzanne, was a French fortress burnt by the English army in 1350.

— *Courcy*: a few km. north of Reims, which was destroyed by 'une chevauchée Anglaise' in 1359. The Black Prince was famous, or notorious, for his cavalry raids.

— *Courmas*: south west of Reims, has a World War I British Army cemetery.

— *Courtisols*: east of Chalons, has one of the longest roadside ribbon developments in France!

— *Gueux*: west of Reims, a village where Churchill met General Eisenhauer in 1944.

— *Hautvillers*: just north of Epernay, was badly damaged by the English army between 1507 and 1537 in Henry VIII's reign.

— *Juvigny*: north west of Chalons, was occupied by Anglo-Burgundian troops in the Hundred Years War.

— *Montmirail*: north west of Sézanne where Napoleon scored an astonishing victory in February 1814 over the Russians and Prussians. A hundred years later the German General Von Bulow briefly occupied the town — for two days.

— *La Neuville aux Larris*: south west of Reims, has a World War I British Army cemetery.

— *Nogent l'Abbesse*: due east of Reims, was a fort used by the Germans in World War I to bombard Reims — for four years!

— *Orbais*: south west of Epernay, was occupied by the English at the end of the Hundred Years War.

— *Poix*: east of Chalons where King Theodore was killed by Attila's troops.

— *Rouvroy Ripont*: north west of Sainte Ménéhould, has the smallest population of any village in Champagne — ten people!

— *St. Hilaire le Grand*: east of Reims, has a chapel, memorial and cemetery for the Russian soldiers who fell in World War I fighting on *this* front, far from home.

— *St. Imoges*: south west of Reims, has a World War I Anglo-French military cemetery.

— *St. Just Sauvage*: south of Sézanne, has a chateau occupied by the English troops in 1356 and again in 1462.

— *Sillery*: this old wine village south of Reims, was burned by the Russians in 1814. The World War I cemetery holds 10,000 tombs of fallen poilus.

— *Souain Perthès lès Hurlus*: halfway between Sainte Ménéhould and Reims. Five little villages were destroyed in World War I. A memorial reads 'Ici fut Perthes'.

— *Witry lès Reims:* just north east of Reims, was occupied for over four years by the Germans in World War I.

CHAPTER ELEVEN: HISTORIC BUILDINGS AND MUSEUMS IN THE MARNE

Since there are so many interesting buildings, mainly churches (and archeological sites) in the Marne, I have listed them alphabetically with notes. They are Monuments Historiques Classées by the French authorities.

Aougny: 25 km. west of Reims just north of the A4 — a good example of 12th century romanesque architecture.

Arcis le Ponsart: Abbey of Igny (3 km. south), just north of Aougny. Founded in 1126 by the monks of Clairvaux, reconstructed at the end of the 18th century.

Baslieux les Fismes: north of Igny. The nave dates from 11th century, tower chevet from the 12th century and transept from the 13th century.

Chalons sur Marne: the cathedral of St. Etienne dates from the 12th century. The treasury contains chalices etc. of the same date. Clovis originally founded it in AD 963 but it was sacked in AD 1138, rebuilt and consecrated by Pope Eugene III in AD 1147. The windows are magnificent, some date from the 13th century.

The eglise Notre Dame en Vaux was founded as early as 7th century and reconstructed in the 12th century. The original cloisters also date from the 12th century, were destroyed in the 18th and rebuilt early 20th century. The church St. Jean is the oldest in Chalons dating from the 11th century with romanesque nave. The church St. Alpin also dates from the 12th century, with delightful 16th century stained glass windows.

Courville: just north of Igny (see above), a romanesque church dating from the 11th century. Statues of wood and stone and a 1519 altar of the style called flamboyant.

L'Epine: a few km. north east of Chalons on the N3. The basilique Notre Dame was constructed in AD 1450, modelled on the two cathedrals of Reims and Chalons. It is a classic flamboyant gothic style and a major pilgrimage site.

Hautvillers: a few km. north of Epernay. The abbey was founded in AD 650 by St. Nivard who installed monks under the rule of St. Benoit and St. Colomban. St. Berchaire was the first Abbot. The relics of Sainte Helène martyred in Rome, the scriptorium and the tomb of Dom Perignon make this an essential visit.

Lagery: just north of Aougny (see above). Pope Urban II who preached the first Crusade in AD 1095, lived there. The main door is 12th century and the nave is 13th century. Frescoes and funeral urns date from the 15th century. In the small champagne village, look at the remains of the medieval chateau and Les Halles.

Lhery: a tiny hamlet almost next door to Lagery. The church dates from the 12th century with beautiful ornate capitals. The tower, chevet and nave date from the 13th century. Nearby is a 15th century chateau with two towers standing.

Magneux: on the N3 just south of Baslieux lès Fismes. The church dates from the 12th century but the transept, traverse and the huge stone altar depicting the Passion date from the 15th century.

Reims:the gothic cathedral of Notre Dame was built during the period 1210–1300 in one huge uncomplicated building. The towers, gallery and gables were added in the 15th century. The eastern facade with three doors, the famous Smiling Angel on the left hand main door and the coloured statue of Joan of Arc are notable sights. Despite considerable damage by the German bombardments in World War I the cathedral has been discreetly restored to its former beauty over 18 years. The golden limestone blocks to build the cathedral were quarried in the Champagne caves from AD 1211 (the wine was *not* sparkling then). The west facade has a gorgeous rose window. Look too for the Chagall windows at the east end and for the tapestries that portray the 'Song of

Songs'. No less than 3,000 Frankish warriors worshipped in the original Christian church of AD 496.

Entry to the cathedral is only from Place de Cardinal Lucon. During the summer months guided tours in English take place (15 francs). Next to the cathedral is the Palais de Tau, a former archiepiscopal palace, so called because of the T shape. The treasury contains King Charles X's coronation robes in gold and velvet, Charlemagne's 9th century talisman and a 12th century chalice from which 20 French kings received their coronation communion. Entry to the two great exhibition halls costs 22 francs but is well worth it, to see one of France's unique treasurehouses.

The Basilique St. Remi is ten minutes walk due east of the cathedral, set in another large paved square (within five minutes walk of several of the champagne shippers' caveaux). Saint Remi was the patron saint of Reims and his body was buried there in AD 533 and is now behind the altar. The main gothic building dates — nave, transepts, vaults etc. — from the 11th century. The facade with towers and chevet date from the 17th century. The basilica is 122 metres long but only 28 metres wide and very tall. Next door is the Abbaye St. Remi, 53 rue St. Simon, the city's main archeological museum (closed on Tuesdays). Buy the 12 franc 'billet commune' for all six Reims museums.

Sainte Ménéhould: 46 km. north east from Chalons, it has the 13th century church of Notre Dame with 15th century organ and stained glass windows on the site of the original chateau. Also have a look at the Hotel de Ville built in 1730 which has a vestibule and staircase of note.

Talus St. Prix: 10 km. north of Sézanne has the magnificent 12th century Abbey of Reclus which was founded by St. Bernard — all in excellent order. Open July and August, not Tuesdays.

Vertus: 20 km. south east of Epernay, has four 12th century vaulted crypts but the main body is mostly 15th century. A champagne town with cave co-operative.

Believe it or not there are another 125 listed churches, mostly of 12th century romanesque architecture, scattered over the

Marne. A few more to note are **Orbais l'Abbaye**, 20 km. south west of Epernay where the original Benedictine abbey was built in the 7th century by St. Réol, Archbishop of Reims. A champagne town, the fête patronale is on Trinity Sunday with floral floats and processions. **St. Amand sur Fion** is north of Vitry le Francois with a really classic gothic 12th century church. **Ay Champagne** has a flamboyant romanesque style church with unusual porch-tower. Besides its dozen champagne shippers and its vignerons co-operatives there is the nearby Grotto of Warmery-Haut and the chateau de la Malmaison. So finally to **Vitry le Francois** 30 km. south east of Chalons to see the Collegiate mainly 17th century church of Notre Dame and the church Charles de Foucauld, the Hotel de Ville, the old house of les Arquebusiers (archers) and the ancient hospital all listed buildings.

If one has to make a limited choice of the vast selection of religious edifices, I would put Reims (1), Chalons (2) and then the cluster of old abbeys due west of Reims.

Chateaux in the Marne

Boursalt: is 10 km. west of Epernay just south of the N4. There are two chateaux here — ancient and modern, the latter built for Madame Clicquot (as in Veuve).

Braux Ste. Cohière: is just west of Sainte Ménéhould. Built in the 17th century it is a quadrilateral brick and stone chateau, a rare example of household cavalry/military style. Tel. 26 60 83 51.

Brugny Vaudancourt: 6 km. south west of Epernay, is a champagne village. The chateau of Brugny was rebuilt in the 16th century but all the towers and most of the walls are 13th century. A vigneron co-operative is nearby.

Dormans: 20 km. west of Epernay on the N3 has a 17th century chateau with two huge 14th century towers. The main logis between two decorated pavilions are of brick and stone. The two neighbouring churches are both listed. There are two vignerons co-operatives and the town fair of St. Crispin is on the last Saturday in October.

Esternay: is 11 km. west of Sézanne off the N4 overlooking the River Grand Morin. Originally built in the 16th century the chateau was in the front line in World War I during the battle of the Marne in August 1914. Visits — telephone 26 42 50 92 and ask for M. de la Rochelambert.

Montmort Lucy: is 17 km. south west of Epernay on the D51. The castle was built in the 12th century and fortified in the 16th century. It has towers, ramparts, moats, drawbridges — an ideal castle to visit. Open for five summer months, closed Mondays. Tel. 26 59 10 04.

Reveillon: a hamlet west of Esternay just north of the N34. Built in the early 17th century the chateau is on the remains of a medieval site. Telephone M. Bruniol de Gineste on 26 42 52 54.

St. Martin d'Ablois: 6 km. south west of Epernay on the D11. The champagne town has a medieval chateau, reconstructed in 1760, now a retirement home.

Other chateaux of note are Etoges (south of Epernay), a classic 16th century chateau, outside only; and Chatillon sur Marne (see the huge statue of Pope Urban II).

Museums

Ay Champagne: Musée Champenois, 4 rue A. France, tel. 26 50 12 57. A wine and vigneron museum. Open every day.

Braux Ste. Cohière: Musée Regional d'Orientation, History of the Pays d'Argonne. Closed Tuesdays. Entry 10 francs. July — September only.

Chalons sur Marne: Musée Municipal, Place Godart. Closed Tuesdays, open afternoons only. Musée Garinet & Goethe Schiller, 13 rue Pasteur/ Closed Tuesdays, open afternoons only. (Battle of Valmy, documents Goethe & Schiller). Musée du Cloitre de Notre Dame en Vaux, rue Nicolas Durand. Closed Tuesdays. Tel. 26 64 03 87. (Archeology). Musée d'Histoire Militaire, 68 rue Leon Bourgeois. Closed Tuesdays, open afternoons only.

Epernay: Musée du Vin de Champagne, de Prehistoire et

d'Archeologie Regionales, 13 Avenue de Champagne, tel. 26 51 90 31. Closed Tuesdays. Entry fee. Closed December — February. Musée Tour de Castellane (Rene Dumont), 57 rue de Verdun, tel. 26 55 15 33. Open May — September. Musée des Pressoirs, Champagne Mercier, 73 Avenue de Champagne, tel. 26 54 75 26. Collection of 35 wine presses. Musée Champenois at Le Mesnil sur Oger, Champagne Launois and at Mussy, at the Auberge Champenoise.

Epine: Musée Agricole de la Bertauge. Tel 26 60 90I 5. Open May — October.

Germaine: Maison du Bucheron, tel. 26 40 43 84. Open March — October, weekends only.

Hautvillers: Histoire de l'Abbaye d'Hautvillers at Moet & Chandon, Epernay.

Giffaumont Chamubert: Grange aux Abeilles (apiculture), tel. 26.41.67.97.

Grigny Eclaires: Maison des Traditions d'Argonne, near Ste. Ménéhould. Open during summer, tel. 26 60 36 34.

Heiltz le Marupt: Folklore Museum, near Sermaize lès Bains. Tel. 26 73 15 16.

Reims: Ancien College de Jesuites, 1 Place Meseux, tel. 26 81 51 50, closed Tuesdays. Chapelle Notre Dame de la Paix, 33 rue du Champ de Mars. Closed Wednesdays. Entry 6 francs. Fort de la Pompelle, N44. Tel. 26 49 11 85. World War I souvenirs. Entry 10 francs. Salle de la Reddition, 12 rue Franklin Roosevelt (German capitulation). Closed Tuesdays. Musée St. Denis, 8 rue Chanzy, tel. 26 47 28 44 (15–16th century paintings etc). Closed Tuesdays. Musée St. Remi, 53 rue Simon, tel. 26 85 23 36 (history and archeology). Afternoons only. Musée Hotel le Vergeur, 36 Place du Forum, tel. 26 47 20 75. (History of Reims). Closed Mondays. Crypto portique gallo-romain, Place du Forum, tel. 26 85 23 26. (Roman Forum). Closed Mondays. Musée de l'Automobile Francaise, 84 Avenue G. Clemenceau, tel. 26 82 84 85 (120 vintage cars).

Sainte Ménéhould: Musée de l'Argonne, Place General Leclerc, tel. 26 60 80 21. Weekend afternoons only.

In the smaller towns ask at the S.I. Tourist Office or Hotel de Ville (Marie) for opening times as they may vary, particularly in the winter out of season.

Towns with half-timbered medieval houses

Chalons sur Marne (many); Reims (9 listed); Sainte Ménéhould, Vitry le François and Giffaumont (La grange aux Abeilles).

Archeological sites

- Chalons sur Marne
- Sainte Marie du Lac
- Valmy
- Verzenay

Natural Wonders

In the forest of Argonne there are many very old oak trees. Le Chêne de Villers was planted in 1637 and le Chêne Napoleon in the forest of Sainte Ménéhould was alive and well in Boney's days. Between Givry and the Charmontois region by the side of the road there are many beech trees in twisted and convoluted shapes (hêtres tordus).

In Baslieux les Fismes there is a petrified fountain of Fontinettes, dolmens at Barbonne Fayel., Fontaine Denis Nuisy, Montmirail, Talus St. Prix and Val des Marais. There are Menhirs at Congy (Pierre Frite) and at Essart lès Sézanne called l'Hermite.

CHAPTER TWELVE:
THE MARNE: FOOD AND BOARD

This is a selection of good value restaurants with a prix fixe menu about 50–60 francs per person excluding wine. The dishes mentioned in brackets are their specialities and are *not* necessarily included in the prix fixe menu.

Ambonnay: Auberge Saint Vincent, 1 rue St. Vincent (Boudin de lapin champenois, Matelotte d'anguille à l'Ambonnay).

Beaumont sur Vesle: La Maison du Champagne, 2 rue du Port (Tripes au champagne, Rognons de veau au ratafia).

Bergeres lès Vertus: Le Mont Aimé, 4 rue de Vertus (Foie gras de canard frais maison, Magret de barbarie au Bouzy).

Chalons sur Marne:
— L'Avenue, 86 Avenue de Sainte Ménéhould (Viandes grillées sur ardoise, Diablotins d'escargots).
— Les Années Folles, 75 rue Leon Bourgeois (Entrecote sauce Roquefort et noix, Magret de canard sauce Périgueux).
— Restaurant l'Accalmie, 16 rue Herbillon (Cuisses de grenouille beurre d'escargots, Escalope cordon bleu).
— Restaurant Le Poelon, 9 rue des Poissoniers (Fondues bourgignons et savoyards).

Chatillon sur Broué: Auberge du Pot Moret (Mousseline de lotte au beurre nantais, Truite aux choix).

Courgivaux: Auberge du Chaperon Rouge, N4 (Truite de mer à l'oseille, Ris de veau aux petits légumes).

Dormans: La Table Sourdet, 6 rue Dr. Moret (Brochet de Marne au beurre blanc. Coq au Vin rouge de Champagne).

Epernay:
— La Terrasse, 7 Quai de la Marne (Foie gras de canard,

Matelotte de rivière au vin d'Ay).
— L'Hermite, 3 Place Mendes France (Grenadin de veau flambé au Porto à la creme d'épinards, Tarte au citron meringuée).

Fère Champenois: La France, 112 rue du Marechal Foch (Ris de veau au champagne, Magret de canard aigre doux).

Fismes: L'Esplanade, 8 rue des Chailleaux (Lapin au marc de champagne, Blanquette de St. Jacques au champagne).

Germaine: Le Relais de la Diligence, Hameau les Haies (Coq au Vin côte de veau champenoise).

La Chaussée sur Marne: Le Midi, rue du Col. Caillot (Entrecote aux morilles, Cassoulet aux confit de canard).

Magenta-Epernay: Chez Max, 13 Avenue Thevenet (Champignons au ratafia).

Montmirail: Le Vert Galant, 2 Place du Vert Galant (Ris de veau braisés, Feuilleté Champenois).

Pleurs (Fère Champenoise):
— La Paix, 4 rue General Leclerc (Foie gras, Choucroute de poissons).
— Le Cheval Gris, 2 rue de la Libèration (Tête de veau au sauce verte).

Reims:
— La Lorraine, 7 Place Drouet d'Erlon (Choucroutes, Confit de canard).
— L'Ancien Pavillon, 2 Boulevard Jules César (Rognons flambés au marc de champagne).
— Le Bignou, 14 Place A. Briand (Filet de boeuf aux morilles, Caille au champagne).
— Le Cornouaille, 217 rue de Barbatre (Filet de barbue en habit vert sauce crevette, Paupiette de saumon aux huitres chaudes).
— The Glue Pot, 49 Place Drouet d'Erlon (Coq au vin rouge, Croustade de ris de veau au champagne).
— Le Paysan, 16 rue de Fismes (Salade au lard ardennaise, Cassoulet à la graisse d'oie).
— Au Tambour, 63 rue de Magneux (Turbot aux fruits de mer, Tortilla montagnarde).

Saint Imoges: Auberge du Bois Joli (Coq au vin, Galette forestière).

Saint Ménéhould:
— Le Cheval Rouge, 1–3 rue Chanzy (Pied de cochon à la Sainte Ménéhould, Tart soufflée aux fruits rouges).
— La Poste (Filet Julienne normande, Magret de canard aux morilles).

Sézanne:
— La Croix d'Or, 53 rue Notre Dame (Terrine de foie gras frais au ratafia, Pêches au champagne).
— Le Relais Champenois et du Lion d'Or, 157 rue Notre Dame (Compote de lapin au romarin, Filet de sole au vin rouge).
— Le Soleil, 17 rue de Paris (Turbot au beurre blanc et aux oeufs de saumon).

Vanault les Dames (nr. Sermaize): La Vanelle, Place de la Mairie (Pintade 'ma facon', Coq au Riesling).

Vauciennes la Chaussée de Damery: Auberge de la Chaussée, 5 Avenue de Paris (Poulet au champagne, Truite au champagne).

Vitry le Francois: Le Gourmet des Halles, 11 rue des Soeurs (Salade Alaska, Filet de daurade en papillotte).

Remember, if the waiter 'forgets' to show you the prix fixe menu, ask him politely but firmly for it! Bon Appetit!

Accommodation

The hotels listed are modest, good value where a double bedroom for the night should not cost more than 100–120 francs *for the room*. Petit déjeuner will be approximately 15–18 francs per person. 'R' indicates le patron has a restaurant, probably with a good meal round about 50 francs including taxes, service but exclusive of wine. Always ask to see your room before you accept it. The price is fixed, i.e. no negotiation and it is marked clearly (a) in the hotel reception and (b) on the back of the bedroom door. You probably will not find any soap and the W.C. will be down the corridor.

Check that the room is not above a noisy street (although after 10.00 p.m. the traffic diminishes as elsewhere).

Hotel   Tel. (26)

Ambonnay 51150,	Auberge St. Vincent, 1 rue St. Vincent	57 01 98 R
Beaumont sur Vesle 51400,	Mourmelon le Grand, 2 rue du Port	03 92 45 R
Bergères lès Vertus 51130,	Le Mont Aimé, 4 rue de Vertus	52 21 31 R
Chalons sur Marne, 51100	Hotel Jolly, 12 rue de la Charrière	68 09 47 —
	Hotel Moritz, 16 rue Lochet	68 09 27 —
	Hotel de la Comédie, 12 Quai Notre Dame	68 10 45 B-R
	Hotel de la Fontaine, 3 rue Leon Bourgeois	68 09 72 —
	Hotel Au Bon Acceuil, 81 rue Leon Bourgeois	68 09 48 —
	Hotel Chemin de Fer, rue de la Gare	68 21 25 R
Chatelraould 51130,	La Petite Auberge	74 01 14 R
Courgivaux 51310 *Esternay,*	Auberge Chaperon Rouge, N4	81 57 09 R
Epernay 51200	La Terrasse, 7 Quai de Marne	55 26 05 R
	Hotel le Progrés, 6 rue des Berceaux	55 22 72 B-R
	Hotel St. Pierre, 1 rue Jeanne d'Arc	54 40 80 —
	Hotel du Nord, 50 rue Edouard Valliant	51 52 65 —
Fere Champenois 51320,	Le Cheval Gris, Pleurs, rue Libération	80 10 20 R
	Hotel le France, 112 rue Foch	42 40 24 R
Fismes 51170,	Hotel l'Esplanade, 8 rue les Chailleaux	78 03 31 R
	Hotel la Gare, 1 Place de la Gare	78 13 82 R
Gaye 51120, Sézanne,	Hotel le Gayon	80 90 75 R
Germaine 51160 Ay,	Le Relais de la Diligence, Hotel des Haies	52 33 69 R
Giffaumont 51290,	Hotel Cheval Blanc	41 62 65 R
Givrey en Argonne 51330,	l'Espérance, Place de la Halle	60 00 08 R
La Chaussée sur Marne 51246,	H. le Midi, rue Col. Caillot	41 94 77 R
Montmirail 51210,	Hot. le Vert Galant, 2 Place Vert Galant	81 20 17 R
Montmort Lucy 51270	Hotel la Place, 3 Place Bertholot	59 10 38 R
	Hotel le Cheval Blanc, Route de Sézanne	59 10 03 R
Mourmelon le Grand 51400,	Hotel les Bruyères, 55 rue General Gourand	66 12 06 —
Pargny sur Saulx 51340,	Hotel à l'Ancre d'Or	73 11 49 R

Pleurs 51230

Fère Champ,	H. la Paix, 4 rue General Leclerc	80 10 14 R
Reims 51100,	L'Ancien Pavillion, 2 Boulevard Jules César	47 63 95 R
	Hotel les Arcades, 16 Passage Subé	47 42 39 —
	Au Bon Acceuil, 31 rue Thilois	88 55 74 —
	Hotel Central, 16 rue Telliers	47 30 08 —
	Hotel le Chateaubriand, 57 rue Thilois	47 50 74 —
	Le Cours Langlet, 53 Cours Langlet	47 13 89 —
	Est Hotel, 222 Avenue Jean Jaurès	07 26 59 —
	Hotel le Monopole, 28 Place Drouet d'Erlon	47 10 33 —
	Le Saint Nicaise, 8 Place St. Nicaise	85 01 26 R
	Hotel le Thillois, 17 rue de Thillois	40 65 65 —
	Hotel Linguet, 14 rue Linguet	47 31 89 —
	Hotel d'Alsace, 6 rue General Sarrail	47 44 08 —
Sainte Ménéhould 51800,	Hotel la Poste, 54 Av. Victor Hugo	60 80 16 R
Saint Imoges,	La Maison du Vigneron de Champagne	51 53 67 R
Sermaize lès Bains 51250,	Hotel des Sports, 12 rue Benard	73 20 77 R
Sézanne 51120,	La Croix d'Or, 53 rue Notre Dame	80 61 10 R
	Le Relais Champenois, 157 rue Notre Dame	80 58 03 R
Tours sur Marne 51150,	La Touraine Champenoise, 2 rue du Pont	59 91 93 R
Vauciennes 51200 Epernay,	Auberge de la Chaussée, 5 Avenue de Paris	58 40 66 R
Ville en Tardenois 51176,	Hotel la Paix	61 81 45 R
Vitry le Francois 51300	Le Bon Séjour, Faubourg Léon Bourgeois	74 02 36 R
	Hotel l'Etoile, 4 Faubourg de Chalons	74 12 56 R
	Hotel du Rondpoint, 28 Avenue République	74 02 84 R
	Hotel Nancy, 22 Grande Rue de Vaux	74 09 37 R
	Nouvel Hotel, 18 rue du Pont	74 03 34 R

Gîtes rureaux

For a list of *Gîtes Ruraux* write to Chambre d'Agriculture, Comp. Ag. du M. Bernard, Route de Suippes, 51009 Chalons sur Marne, Cedex or Tel. 26 64 08 13. A brief summary follows.

There are three basic categories. Gîtes de France or Gîtes Rureaux are holiday homes in the countryside or in the mountains, perhaps in a village or part of a farm. They are fully furnished, equipped for a family to move in and are usually charged for by the week.

The Chambre d'Hôte is the equivalent of bed and breakfast in the UK but in France is usually in the countryside, in a farm and offers overnight accommodation. The evening meal should be negotiated with the owner.

Les Gîtes Camping are small campsites on farmland for campers and caravanners. Drinking water, showers, wash basins, toilets and washing facilities for clothes are provided.

In the Marne, 70 small villages offer gîtes facilities. The Gîtes Ruraux prices in mid-summer range between 500–900 francs per week per family. Chambre d'hôte prices for a *couple* are in the 110–120 franc range and the table d'hôte (evening meal) is in the range 45–60 francs per person. The Gîte Camping prices range from 8–15 francs per adult per day with half price for children.

Municipal camps

The municipal camp sites are at:
- Anglure 51260 (tel. 42 71 51)
- Chalons sur Marne 51000 (tel. 68 38 00)
- Chatillon/Broué 51290 St. Remy en Bouzemont (tel. 72 60 21)
- Conflans sur Seine 51260, Anglure (tel. 42 61 59)
- Connantre 51230 Fère Champenoise (tel.81 08 76)
- Courgivaux 51310 Esternay (tel. 81 58 54)
- near Chateau Courgivaux 51310 Esternay (by the lake) (tel. 81 58 54)
- Dormans 51700 (tel. 58 21 45)
- Epernay 51200 (tel. 56 32 14)
- Fismes 51170 (tel. 78 10 26)
- Giffaumont Champaubert 51290 (tel. 72 61 84)
- Givry en Argonne 51330 (tel. 60 01 97)
- Mareuil le Port 51700, Minaucourt 51800, Sainte Ménéhould (tel. 60 40 17)
- Montmirail 51210 (tel. 81 25 61)
- Reims 51100 (Avenue Hoche) (tel. 85 41 22)
- Sainte Ménéhould 51800 (tel. 60 80 21)

- St. Remy en Bouzemont 51290 (tel. 72 62 85)
- Sarcy 51170 Fismes (tel. 97 43 60)
- Sézanne 51120 (tel. 80 57 00)
- Thieblemont Faremont 51300 (tel. 73 81 03)
- Val de Vesle 51400 Mourmelon le Grand (tel. 03 91 79)
- Vitry le Francois 51300 (tel. 74 07 24)
- Villers sous Chatillon 51700 Dormans (tel. 58 33 02)

Prices vary considerably. Sézanne is the cheapest at 3.10 francs per adult per day to Braucourt and Thieblemont Faremont at 11 francs per day.

CHAPTER THIRTEEN:
THE AUBE — NOTABLE TOWNS
AND VILLAGES

The Aube (Michelin Map 61) is shaped as a perfect quadrilateral nearly 80 km. (50 miles) along each border — the Marne departement being to the north, Haute Marne to the east, Côte d'Or and Yonne in the Burgundy region respectively south and west. The préfecture town of Troyes (population 7,000) is plumb in the centre on the River and Canal of the Seine. The two sub-préfecture towns are Nogent sur Seine (population 5,000) west north west of Troyes (50 km.) and Bar sur Aube (population 7,300) to the east of Troyes, also about 50 km. distance. The population of 300,000 and land area of 6,000 sq. km. make the Aube an underpopulated and relatively unknown region.

The other towns are Romilly sur Seine (population 17,400) 20 km. east of Nogent sur Seine, la Chapelle Saint Luc (population 15,000) a few km. north west of Troyes, Sainte Savine (population 10,500) a few km. west of Troyes and Bar sur Seine (population 3,200) 30 km. south east of Troyes.

The Rivers Aube, the Seine and their tributaries, water the departement and 12 km. due east of Troyes is the large lake 'la Foret d'Orient'. I have an interest to declare about the Aube. When my Gascon forbears were forced out of Aquitaine they came via the Auvergne, the Aube and Paris to London.

For me the two great attractions of the Aube departement are the exquisite medieval 'city' of Troyes with its nine classified churches and medieval quarter and the interesting secondary Champagne area around Bar sur Aube. In addition, there are many excellent castles (once vassals of the Comte de Champagne) at Ville Hardouin, Dampierre, Rumilly Vermoise

115

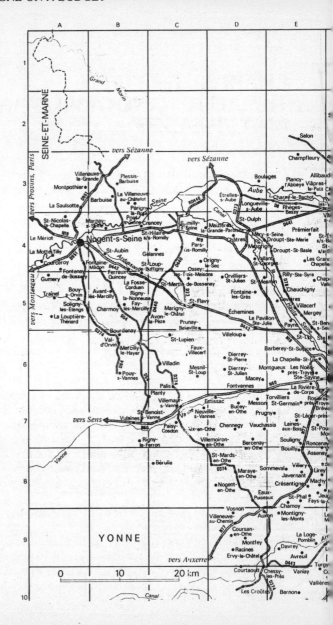

THE AUBE – NOTABLE TOWNS AND VILLAGES

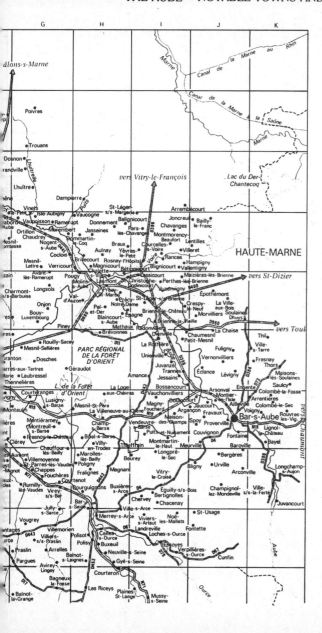

of the 16th century and rather grander ones of the 17th and 18th century at Villemereuil, Vendeuvre Dampierre, Brienne and la Motte Tilly. For cider lovers the Pays d'Othe offers a quality drink and Les Riceys produces one of the best rosé wines in France.

As before, the major city of the departement is featured first and then by region based on the leading town in that area, i.e. Troyes, Nogent sur Seine and Bar sur Aube.

Troyes

One arrives at Troyes from the north (Chalons sur Marne 77 km.) on the N77 from the north east (Nancy 186 km.) on the D960, from the east (Chaumont 94 km. or Bar sur Aube 52 km.) on the N19, from the south east (Dijon 152 km.) on the N71, the south west (Auxerre 81 km.) or the west (Sens 65 km.) on the N60. The main roads from Paris, Sézanne (60 km.), Nogent sur Seine (56 km.) are the N19 and N319 coming from the west north west. No wonder it was the historical capital of the Champagne region and of the Counts of Champagne and its famous trade fairs attracted merchants in the Middle Ages from all over Europe. During the Renaissance, Troyes became one of France's centres of the Arts, specifically of stained glass manufacture and sculpture (and then later bonneterie, hat/cap/bonnet/beret manufacture). The Counts of Champagne encouraged the Jewish community which helped not only Troyes' prosperity but its reputation for culture.

The origins of Troyes (pronounced Trois) followed the familiar pattern. The benevolent Roman occupation absorbed the Gallic tribe of Tricasses and the town was then called Augustobona after Emperor Augustus. Evangelised in the 3rd century, St. Loup the most famous of the early bishops (53 years wearing his mitre), offered himself as hostage in AD 451 to Attila in order to save the city. Attila had already sacked Reims and it was in the nature of a miracle that Bishop St. Loup persuaded the Hun not to do the same to Troyes.

When the Romans withdrew to their own country, the Normans predictably devastated Troyes. The worthy citizens rebuilt and under the Counts of Champagne the city enjoyed prosperity in the early Middle Ages, even though the town was burnt almost to the ground in AD 1188. The two great trading Fairs were called the 'chaude' on St. John's Day of 24th June or the 'froide' on St. Rémi's Day of 1st October. The two Counts of Champagne of particular fame were Henri I under whose auspices 13 churches and 13 hospitals were built in Troyes circa 1200 and his grandson, Thibaut IV, mid-13th century, who was a 'beau chevalier', poet and sponsored Christian de Troyes, the great romantic writer/poet.

When Jeanne, Countess of Champagne, married Philippe le Bel, King of France, in AD 1284, the province of Champagne as her dowry was absorbed into the kingdom. The Hundred Years War between France and England caused the usual hardships to the region, particularly since their powerful southern neighbours, the Burgundian counts, allied themselves to the English kings. Queen Isabel of France signed the Treaty of Troyes with England on 21st May 1420 in Troyes and her daughter Catherine married our King Henry V in the church of St. Jean. Our history books say that this was a logical and sensible marriage to link the two great countries. Not so, to the French. This marriage and Treaty has always been designated as 'honteux', i.e. shameful. Joan of Arc opened the gates of Troyes to Charles VII on 9th July 1429 to greet him before they went to Reims for his coronation.

After the English left the country Troyes saw prosperity again until a fire devoured most of the town on 24th May 1524. From the middle of the 18th century the growth of 'la bonneterie' produced the prosperity lost when the great fairs ceased. Now nearly 20,000 people and 300 producers in and around Troyes are involved in the production of hosiery and other knitted products. The town is twinned with Chesterfield in Derbyshire.

Troyes has two distinct districts. The champagne cork shape has the head facing north east bounded almost completely by the River Seine and the Seine canal. Inside this semicircle, called 'la Cité', is the cathedral, the Museum of Modern Art, alongside it the Museum of St. Loup and the 18th century pharmacy of the Hotel Dieu. There are several parks and well

119

laid out streets and the surrounding river and canal make la Cité an agreeable place in which to stroll and observe.

The main cylinder of the champagne cork is about 800 metres in depth by 600 metres in width. This sector is called Le Bourg (town). The Bourg is much as it would have been in the 16th and 17th centuries. Narrow streets with four or even five floors, gabled roofs and half-timbered houses. (Look for la Tourelle de l'Orfevre, la Maison du Boulanger). The streets to visit are clustered around the churches of St. Jean, Sainte Madeleine, St. Remy, St. Urbain and others. Please do visit the Place du Marechal Foch, rue Champeaux, ruelle des Chats, Cour de Mortier d'Or, rue de Valuisant and rue du General Saussier (where there is an excellent little restaurant). Also the Hotel des Chapelaines, Maison des Allemands, Place du Marché au Pain and Hotel de Marisy.

There are two tourist offices, one at the south west end by the SNCF, the other near the Canal of the Seine between the church of St. Urbain and the Museum of the Hotel Dieu. Guided tours between July and September are essential because there are so many historical nooks and crannies which are impossible to discover without the local specialist guide to show you. See Chapter Fourteen for descriptions of the cathedral and museums.

There are plenty of good value hotels and restaurants in Troyes. The Festival Populaire of music, ballet, theatre and art exhibitions is held from the middle of June for four weeks. The modern commercial Fair of Champagne takes place in June. The main fête day is that of St. Jean on the 14th July.

Excursions are many and varied out of Troyes. To the east is the huge Regional Park and lake 'La Foret d'Orient' (see Chapter Nineteen). The circuit starts on the Avenue 1er Mai, then N19 signed for Bar sur Aube. The road runs parallel with canals feeding into the lake.

Eastern circuit

— *Mesnil St. Père* is 21 km. along the N19 and is the southern village with good beaches and boating on the edges of the 2,300 hectares of lake water.

— *Vendeuvre sur Barse* 10 km. further on has a listed chateau, a 16th century church and specialises in andouillettes (pig products) and 'bonneterie'.

— *Thieffrain* just south, was occupied by the English army in the Hundred Years War.

Take the D443 north for 8 km. to *Amance* on the eastern edge of the oak forests. Sangliers (wild boar) and cerfs (deer) abound.

To *Dienville* and *Brienne le Chateau* (population 4,000). The powerful Counts of Brienne have a fascinating history. In the Crusades they married into the family of the Kings of Sicily, were close friends of the various popes and one of them, Jean I, became King of Jerusalem, then Emperor of Constantinople. They were 'la fleur de la noblesse de Champagne'. Alas the reigning son was killed in 1356 at Poitiers by the English chivalry.

Later on the young Napoleon Bonaparte studied at the military academy of Brienne. One of his lesser Marshals, Valée, was born and bred at Brienne. There are four good little hotel/restaurants here and the café/restaurant Napoleon. The local speciality is Choucroute de Champagne. See Chapter Fifteen for the chateau and museum.

North of Brienne there are some villages of interest with English links, on the D6. For instance *Montmorency Beaufort* was once owned by the English. Blanche of Artois, the widow of Henri III (the last Count of Champagne), married the Count of Lancaster, Edmond of England. Then their grand-daughter, Blanche of Lancaster, married John of Gaunt, son of King Edward III. For over a century this region belonged to the English royal family.

Chavanges was owned by the same family and the fête patronale is that of St. George. *Lentilles* was part of the same fief and has a notable 16th century church.

Rosnay l'Hopital on the D396 has a listed church (see Chapter Fourteen) which was consecrated by St. Thomas à Becket, then in exile at Pontigny in northern Burgundy. The village was the scene of a miracle by St. Bernard on 5th February 1147. Rather later Marshal Marmont held the

Bavarian army at bay here to protect Napoleon's retreat on 2nd February 1814.

The N60 is 39 km. back to Troyes. An airport and a museum on the right, then *Lesmont,* across the River Aube, and 9 km. to *Piney* (a quick look at the Place de la Halle — covered market). The local speciality is potée champenoise, a splendid meat stew.

Just to the south is *Géraudot* the village at the north end of the Lac de la Foret d'Orient. A major ornithological game reserve is on the D43 near Géraudot.

Back on the N60 through *Mesnil Sellières* and *Créney.* Here spare a glance at the monument to 49 members of the Resistance shot by the modern Hun on 22nd August 1944. The 12th century church is listed. So back in to Troyes.

Southern circuit

The southern circuit from Troyes starts on the N71 via — *Breviandes* parallel to the River Seine and *Buchères*, where on 24th August 1944 the 51st SS Regiment murdered 66 men, women and children.

— *Verrières* 2 km. to the east, across the river where my ancestor Philippe de la Force owned the commune of St. Aventin in the first half of the 18th century. Keep on the N71.

— At *Rumilly les Vaudes* 3 km. to the south, is a notable listed chateau and church.

From *Fouchères, Vitry sur Bar* to *Bar sur Seine* (population 3,200) which is one of the prettiest villages around Troyes. It has many timbered 16th century houses, a clock tower, a 17th century town gate, remains of a 12th century chateau and 12th century Templar chapel (Avaleur).

Pilgrimages take place on the 8th September at Notre Dame du Chêne 2 km. south west. Andouillettes, river trout and gougères are the local specialities. There is an open air theatre in June. Visit too, the champagne wine co-operative. There are so many fish in the nearby river l'Ource, l'Arce and la Laignes that fishing permits are issued without any restrictions (very rare indeed). Monsieur and Madame Puissant at the hotel/restaurant du Commerce, 30 rue de la Republique, will give you a good meal of Champagne cuisine.

Keep on the N71 to *Polisy*. In the Middle Ages, Jean IV de Polisy was ambassadeur at the London Court. He constructed the Chateau in the angle formed by the two rivers Seine and the Laigne in 1543–44.

The D542 leads via *Bainot* (Chateau Treuffet) 8 km. to *Les Riceys* (population 1,500) which is well known for its excellent vin rosé. Louis XIV made it his favourite wine. The town has always been in the firing line by vandals. Normans and the English in the Hundred Years War but in addition it was on the frontier between Burgundy and Champagne. The local champagne firms are Noirot and Marquis de Pomereuil (tel. 29 32 24). The three Riceys (Bas, Haute Rive and Haut) all have churches, dovecotes, cellars, stables and parks of interest. Definitely worth a look at the chateau (see Chapter Fifteen).

The D17 heads west via *Bagneux la Fosse* a champagne village taking its name from the Roman spa baths from the River Sarce. See Chateau Michel Baujean.

Next 11 km. to *Pargues* (windmill and church) and 6 km. to *Chaource* (population 1,000). This is a 'village fleuri' and the fête de muguet (Lily of the valley)is on 1st May. Besides an outstanding church, the village is well known for its cheeses. Try them at the hotel/restaurant Bouvard (tel. 40 12 81).

There are several 'fromageries' including Hugerot and le Panier Champenois. The cheese fair is on the third Sunday in October. Chaource is surrounded on all sides by huge forests.

Drive north on the D444 through the forest of Crogny and of Aumont. *Villemereuill* on the left has a handsome Louis XVIII chateau and *Moussey* a chateau and 12th century church. *Isle Aumont* on the right has a romanesque church with a striking collection of sarcophagi. Then back on the N71 into Troyes.

South western tour

— The south western tour from Troyes starts at the town of *Sainte Savine* (population 10,600) on the N60 which is in effect the western suburb of Troyes. A young Christian Greek girl from Samos called Savinien was martyred by the Roman legions. Her twin sister Maximiniole came from the isle of Samos to look for Savine and arrived at the gates of Troyes in January AD 288. Learning of her sister's martyrdom, she too died of sorrow and was buried alongside her twin. During World War I there was founded the Scottish Women's Hospital for the Allied wounded.

The listed buildings include a Celtic tomb called la Croix la Beigne, a 16th century church and a museum in the Hotel de Ville. The gastronomic specialities include the manufacture of nougat, of cheese and of andouillette (fairs in September).

The N60 continues west through *Fontvannes* to *Estissac* (population 1,800), a charming village on the edge of the Forest of Othe, where the Roman general beat Attila in AD 451, which was called the Battle of the Catalaunic fields. Salmon breeding in the River Vanne is the local speciality.

Keep on the N60 to *Villemaur sur Vanne* which was once a fortified town. Now 19 more or less ruined towers, walls and moats can still be seen. The 12th century church is a gem (see Chapter Fifteen).

Just beyond a huge silo turn left and south on the D374 to *Paisy Cosdon* and *Aix en Othe* (population 2,300). Once a Roman spa town (Aix = aguae), there are still remains of aqueducts, a 16th century church, and the sad cemetery of Huguenots (my family were 16th and 17th century Huguenots). The auberge de la Jeiern at la Vove will give you a good lunch.

— Next *Villemoiron en Othe* — we are now on the 'route du cidre' — in apple growing country. *St. Mards en Othe* which was the scene of a bloody fight between the Resistance and the Germans on 20th June 1944, then to *Maraye en Othe* and *Eaux Puiseaux* to *Auxon* (with 16th century church).

— Six km. south west to *Villeneuve au Chemin*. This village was owned in the 16th century by the Scottish family of Cockburn (as in Port wine) although it is gallicised now to

Cockborne. In the 12th century village church are two gravestones and funeral urns with the arms of Adam Cockburn. Pilgrimages are made to the nearby Chapel of St. Joseph in May and August.

— The D22 heads south east 8 km. to *Ervy le Chateau* (population 1,200). The town gatehouse Porte St. Nicholas, the covered market, a lovely 16th century church and a collection of statues make this a good stop. Try the hotel/restaurant Franco-Belge, then walk along the boulevards, along the original ramparts.

— Take the D72 east to *Basse Vacherie, Davrey, La Coudre* north to *Montigny les Monts* on to the main road N77 signed for Troyes. At *Villery* in AD 493 the Christian King Clovis met his bride-to-be, Clotilde. *Bouilly* (population 1,000) and *Souligny* where the listed church and the local wines are better than usual and via *St. Germain* into Troyes.

— To the north west of Troyes there are several sites of interest. *Barberey St. Sulpice* has a superb Louis XIII style chateau, *Arcis sur Aube* (3,400), the town where Danton was born and lived and Balzac wrote some novels. Here Napoleon fought his last battle at Arcis (before Waterloo). It was badly bombed by the Germans in 1940.

Nogent sur Seine

Nogent sur Seine (population 5,100) is the sub-prefecture town 51 km. north east of Troyes on the D442. Being on a navigable part of the River Seine, Nogent has always been a 'port fluvial' with barge traffic and a century or two back, the floating of wood downstream towards Paris. The cereal crops of the Champagne countryside were also shipped downriver. Now it is a pleasant town with many half-timbered houses in the old quarter, including the maison Henry IV, the maison Turque, the maison Bertin (where Napoleon stayed in February 1814) and the maison de Gustave Flaubert.

The church of St. Laurent, 15th century with a renaissance campanile, is noted in Chapter Fifteen, as is the museum of

125

Paul Dubois and Alfred Bouchet. In the background are the windmills, granary silos and a huge nuclear central electricity plant and two towers. Nogent produces 2,600 megawatts of electricity and is one of the principal electricity producers in France.

A small chapel 'du Dieu de Pité' on the south side of town has an inscription 'Frux fuit hic bellum nostraetes inter et anglos 25 Juin 1359'. This commemorates the battle between the French troops of Charles V against the English garrison of Nogent under the command of Eustache d'Auberchicourt. In February 1814 the Allied troops defeated Napoleon's army at Nogent and the town was burnt. Try the hotel/restaurant Beau Rivage (tel. 39 84 22) where M. Philippe Chansard will serve you Champagne specialities.

Our King Henry VI owned much of the countryside including *Perigny la Rose* and *Etrelle sur Aube. La Motte Tilly* (see Chapter Fifteen) is a magnificent 18th century chateau 3 km. south west on the west side of the D951. One of the finest in Champagne. Abelarde and Héloise's Abbey of Paraclet is in the village of *St. Aubin* 6 km. south east of the N19 and D442. Sadly there is not much left to see — cellars, a chapel and an obelisk.

Eastern tour

— To the east along the N19 is *Pont sur Seine* which was called in Charlemagne's days 'Douze Ponts'. Napoleon offered the chateau to 'Madame Mère' who lived in it for many years. An aqueduct, the chateau and a listed church are to be found here.

— Keep east on the N19 through *Crancey* (a pretty bridge and stone washing tank-lavoir), *St. Hilaire sur Romilly* to *Romilly sur Seine* (population 17,400) — a town made prosperous by the SNCF workshops, the 'bonneterie' business, textiles and cereal co-operatives.

— The Abbey of Sellières is just to the west of the town. There are four hotel/restaurants — try the Champagne, 10 rue de la Boule d'Or. The town is twinned with Milford Haven in the UK.

Northern tour

— *Villenaux la Grande* (population 1,800) is a champagne village 15 km. north of Nogent. Ceramics, faience and porcelain are made here.

— The old abbey of *Nesle* 3 km. north, is now a school, but the 13th century church is classified. The old timbered houses (pans de bois), presbytère and windmills make the village of interest — try the hotel/restaurant du Chateau known for its river trout (tel. 21 31 66).

Bar sur Aube

Bar sur Aube (population 7,200) is the second sub-prefecture town (Michelin Map 61) 52 km. east of Troyes on the N19 and 24 km. south east of Brienne le Chateau. In the Middle Ages one of the six great trade fairs of Champagne took place here — it was also an important salt storehouse which meant that traders had to visit the town to buy their supplies.

It is not an elegant town but it combines busy activity with a saucy charm. There are a dozen old half-timbered houses, many of them 16th century including one where the Emperor Alexandre of Russia and Frederick of Prussia lodged in 1814, and another which Marshall Joffre used as his headquarters during the September 1914 Battle of the Marne. The 12th century church of St. Macou is classified (see Chapter Fifteen).

The town has the River Aube on the south side and a canal forming a rectangle along the other three sides. There are several fêtes — patronal on Palm Sunday — the daffodil (jonquil) fête in April — the pilgrimage of Sainte Germaine on the 1st May. On the second Sunday in September is the Foire aux Vins de Champagne since Bar sur Aube is the centre of the southern Champagne area.

There are wine co-operatives in the town and a tasting (wooden) cave on the N19 on the east side of town. There are five hotels to choose from. The Commerce is the best but the Pomme d'Or and the St. Nicolas are good value.

Wine tour

Before we set off on a delicious wine tour, the basic facts are that the Aube produces about 18–20% of the total from 3,600 hectares (9,000 acres) in a 15 x 60 km. area. The average wine farm is 1½ hectares (nearly 4 acres). The grape varieties are the same, Pinot Noir, Pinot Meunier and the white Chardonnay. The chalky soil and the weather are about the same as the more famous areas north of Reims, Epernay and Ay. There are 56 wine villages crammed into the area with Bar sur Aube, Essoyes, Les Riceys and Bar sur Seine being the most important (but not necessarily the best) areas.

An interesting circuit starts east on the N19 on the Chaumont road but shortly turn right and south east on the D396 over the River Aube and the railway to *Bayel* (population 1,300). In Louis XIV's reign a Venetian Senor Mazzolay, set up a factory to make glass crystal products. The Cie. Francaise de Cristal was formed in 1666. The local sand and silica were ideal for the purpose and Minister Colbert was well pleased (and so presumably was Louis XIV). The crystal factory is open for visits every day.

The D396 follows the River Aube southwards through the forest of Clairvaux. Here in AD 1115 St. Bernard asked our Stephen (Etienne) Harding, Abbot of Citeaux, to found the Abbey which became one of the shining stars of Christendom. Sadly (as at Cluny and Citeaux) the ravages of mortal man have left only a modicum of the grandeur, but do try to see what is left and think of what it was like eight centuries ago.

The D12 is a straight road to the west through the forest to Champignol lèz Mondeville, then south west to *St. Usage* (see Champagne Bartnicki), *Fontette* (Chateaux Senez and René l'Huillier — co-operative des vignerons) to *Essoyes*, a small fortified village where Auguste Renoir lived part of his life and is buried — a champagne village (see Chateau Senez who have 12 hectares under production).

Then *Loches sur Ource* which has January fêtes of St. Vincent and St. Jean to *Landreville* and north to *Viviers sur Artout*, *Chacenay* (all champagne producing villages), *Bertignolles*, *Eguilly sur Bois*, *Vitry le Croisé* (where the farm of Fontarce was built before AD 1147 by the monks of Clairvaux), *Bligny*, where there is a chateau and M. Lorin of Chateau de Bligny who owns 17 hectares of vineyards will show you his sparkling wines.

On the D4 turn right over the River Landion to *Urville* where there is Chateau Drappier and a wine co-operative. East to *Arconville* and visit Bernard Gaucher, north to *Baroville* (Chateau Barfontare with another wine co-operative) and via the D70 and D396 back into Bar sur Aube.

At Essoyes you could make a detour south south east to four wine villages on the Seine. *Mussy* (population 1,700), a curious little medieval fortified village with a history of recent Resistance in 1944, a chateau, 13th century listed church, a museum of the Resistance and Chateau Herard et Fluteau, a small quality grower. The other villages are *Neuville* (Paul Herard), *Courteron* (Fleury), *Gyé sur Seine* (Cheurlin et Fils and Clerambault), *Buxeuil* (Leblond) and *Celles sur Ource* (Marcel Vezien).

There is a similar circuit out of Bar sur Aube initially south west to Couvignon, Meurville (a champagne co-operative), north on the D44 to Spoy (a listed Roman bridge) through the woods to Argancon Dolancourt which was owned by the monks of Clairvaux and was badly damaged in the 1814 battles (the honey is good here) then turn left on the main road to Maison Neuve.

Just to the east, Arsonnal has a listed church and a small museum with the Loukine icons. Plenty of wild boar around too (sangliers). Our objective is *Soulaines Dhuys* reached by the D113 to Levigny and the D384 north for 9 km. The former was owned by the English royal family (see Montmorency Beaufort). The chateau of Villemahen, several medieval gabled houses and a 16th century listed church make this village worth a detour.

Then due east along the D960 to Tremilly and south to Thil, Thors where there is a factory which makes tin toy soldiers, Saulcy to Colombe le Sec (Chateau Charles Clement) where the Clairvaux Abbey owned vast storehouses. It is still listed as a monument historique as is the 12th century church. A champagne co-operative is in the village, as there is in Colombe la Fosse and Rouvres les Vignes.

Now for the objective of this circuit — General de Gaulle's home village and last resting place at *Colombey lès Deux Eglises* (which is technically 3 km. inside the neighbouring departement of Haute Marne). You will see first of all the huge rose coloured granite memorial cross of Lorraine on the hilltop overlooking the village towering 45 metres above the landscape. On the east side of the hill is the village. The 12th century church Notre Dame en Son Assumption has magnificent choir stalls and a crenellated romanesque tower. The Musée de la Boisserie is where the General made his home for three decades. A very great, but difficult man — R.I.P.

Guided tours

The Champagne negociant shippers of the Aube who will give the individual, and certainly groups, a professional tour and visit to their caves are listed below.

	Tel (prefix 25)
Laurent, 10110 Celles sur Ource	38 50 10
Réné Jolly, 10 rue de la Gare, 10110 Landreville	38 50 91
André Drappier, 10200 Urville	26 40 15
Co-op. Vinicole Defontsoyes, 10360 Fontette	29 60 63
Jean Guerinot, 10300 Montgueux	74 84 76
Alex Bonnet, 138 rue du Gen. de Gaulle, 10340 Les Riceys	29 30 93
Léonze d'Albe Ucavic, Domaine Villeneuve, 10110 Bar sur Seine	38 85 57
Marcel Vezien, rue de la Lande, 10110 Celles sur Ource	38 50 22
Robert Dufour, 4 rue de la Croix Malot, 10110 Landreville	38 52 25
Co-op. Vinicole Côteaux de l'Arce, Ville sur Arce, 10110 Bar sur Seine	38 74 07
Cheurlin & Fils, 13 rue de la Gare, 10250 Gyé sur Seine	38 20 27
Bernard Tassin, 46 Grande Rue, 10110 Celles sur Ource	38 50 19
Cellier de Colombe le Sec 10200	27 02 04

Nearly all offer free tasting facilities. It would, therefore, be polite to buy a few bottles. Try to phone in advance if you can.

The local Aube Confrèries (the jolly companions) are:

1. Confrèrie des Vignerons Aubois (M. Lassaigne Berlot) 10300 Montgueux.
2. Commanderie du Saulte Bouchon, (M. Vezien), Celles sur Ource, 10110 Bar sur Seine.
3. Confrèrie du Taste Cidre, (M. Besancon), Vaujurennes Paisy Cosdon 10160, Aix en Othe.
4. Confrèrie St. Paul St. Vincent, (M. Breuzon), Colombe le Sec, 10200 Bar sur Aube.

If you have a week to spend in the Aube departement I would suggest two or three days in Troyes, a day in Nogent, another at Brienne le Chateau and two at Bar sur Aube (wine tours and a visit to General de Gaulle's village of Colombey lès Deux Eglises).

CHAPTER FOURTEEN: HISTORIC BUILDINGS AND MUSEUMS IN THE AUBE

Following the same format as in Chapter Eleven, I have listed the three main categories: churches/cathedrals/abbeys; chateaux; museums, in separate categories in alphabetical order. Troyes is such a treasure house that reading about its gems 'en masse' is a little indigestible.

Main ecclesiastical buildings

The two abbeys to see (or their remains) are Clairvaux, near Ville sous le Ferté and Le Paraclet. At Clairvaux there is a free guided tour on the first Saturday in the month (April — October) at 3.15 p.m., lasting for two hours. (Tel. 25 26 20 08). Le Paraclet, 10400 Nogent sur Seine, founded by Abelard with Hèloise as the first Abbesse, has free visits every day (afternoons only) July — September inclusive. (Tel. 25 39 79 56).

Aix en Othe: 40 km. west of Troyes. Two 16th century churches and the chapel of St. Avit.

Arcis sur Aube: 40 km. north of Troyes. 15th century church.

Auxon: 30 km. south west of Troyes. 16th century church, Renaissance doors.

Bar sur Aube: 12th century church of St. Maclou and of St. Pierre, Ursuline convent.

Bar sur Seine: 16th century church St. Etienne, Notre Dame du Chêne chapel. Templar chapel at Avallur, mainly 12th century gothic style.

Bérulle: 45 km. south west of Troyes, 16th century gothic style church.

Bouilly: 20 km. south west of Troyes, flamboyant gothic style 16th century church.

Brienne le Chateau: 12th century church and of course, much else to see.

Brienne la Vieille: (3 km. south) Church St. Pierre ès Liens, mainly 12th century and Roman cloisters.

Chaource: 30 km. south of Troyes, the church of St. John the Baptist, mainly 12th century, has magnificent 'Mise au Tombeau' frescoes, 16th century wooden crêche, stained glass windows and ranks as one of the finest churches in Champagne.

Chappes: 30 km. south east of Troyes, a mainly 12th century romanesque church.

Charmont sous Barbuise: 20 km. north of Troyes, 16th century church.

Chavanges: 15 km. north of Brienne, 12th century church but reconsecrated 14th October 1554.

Dampierre: 50 km. north west of Brienne, 12th century church and good 17th century chateau.

Evry le Chatel: 35 km. south west of Troyes, the 15th century church of St. Pierre ès Liens has lovely stained glass windows (see the sybilles), statues, painted panels — well worth a visit.

Fouchères: 30 km. south east of Troyes, a 12th century church, mausoleum and chateau.

Isle Aumont: 10 km. south of Troyes is one of the finest archaeological sites in the Aube. The 12th century church of St. Pierre, with romanesque chapel inside, wooden statue, furnishings and merovingian necropolis. Well worth a visit.

Lentilles: 30 km. north east of Brienne, half timbered 16th century church.

Lhuitre: 35 km. north east of Troyes, 12th century church and chapel of Sainte Tanche.

Luyères: 12 km. north east of Troyes, 15th century church, notable rood screen.

Montiéramey: 15 km. south east of Troyes, 12th century church.

Mussy sur Seine: 35 km. south west from Bar sur Aube, 13th century church.

Neuville sur Seine: 30 km. south west from Bar sur Aube, large statue of Notre Dame des Vignes of 1864 holding a bunch of grapes and imploring heaven for protection for the vines.

Nogent sur Seine: the 15th century church of St. Laurent, the choir and transept were built in 1321, the nave in 1500 and the huge tower in 1521. *Pont sur Seine* (near Nogent) has a 12th century church.

Pont Sainte Marie: 4 km. east of Troyes. A 16th century church with three naves, statues, stained glass windows, fortified tower — all flamboyant and Renaissance. Worth a visit.

Les Riceys: equidistant 35 km. south east/south west from Troyes and Bar sur Aube. Each of the three big communes (Bas, Hauterre and Haut) have 15th or 16th century listed churches.

Rosnay l'Hopital: 10 km. north of Brienne, has a 12th century church and the AD 1270 crypt dedicated by Thomas à Becket. Well worth a visit.

Sainte Savine: 3 km. west of Troyes, 16th century church with 7th century tomb of Ragnegisilus, Bishop of Troyes.

Savières: 15 km. north west of Troyes, 12th century Romanesque church.

Trouans: 40 km. north of Troyes, 12th century church of Trouan le Grand.

Troyes:
— St. Peter & St. Paul's cathedral, 13–15th century, was built in 1208 in Gothic style, consecrated in 1430 and finally completed in 1638. One of the largest cathedrals in France, with brilliant rose windows and 13th century stained glass windows. The rich Treasury holds the psalters and alms-boxes of the Counts of Champagne. Sainte Madelaine,

mid-12th century, is the oldest church in Troyes, late Romanesque with Renaissance steeple. Its rood loft, a marvel of lacy stonework, was carved by Jean Gailde in the 16th century. The chevet stained glass windows are of the school of Champagne.

— St. Jean was built in the 13th century and partly destroyed by fire in 1524. See the curious octagonal clock tower and several wall paintings of note inside. In 1420 King Henry V married Catherine of France here.

— St. Remy is partly 14th century, mainly 15–16th century. The steeple, built in 1386 has a 60 metre high wooden spire, clad in slates, flanked by four bell turrets.

— St. Nicholas was destroyed by fire in 1524 and then rebuilt in Renaissance style with stained glass windows and statues of the Troyes school.

— St. Nizier is 16th century with beautiful stained glass windows.

— The Basilique St. Urbain was founded by Pope Urban IV of Champagne. It is gothic style in the period 1262–70 with 13th century stained glass windows and many impressive statues. The basilique is probably even more impressive than the cathedral. Saint Pantaleon was built in 1516 and burnt down eight years later! It was rebuilt in Renaissance style by 1672 and there are statues and stained glass windows of note.

— St. Martin in the western suburbs, was built in 1592 with a twin domed steeple, beautiful stained glass windows by Linard Gontier.

Villemaure sur Vanne: 35 km. west of Troyes, has a 13th century church with lovely rood screen.

Villeneuve au Chatelot: 12 km. north east of Nogent has a 12th century fortified church.

Villeneuve au Chatelot: 12 km. north east of Nogent has a 12th century fortified church.

Villemaure sur Vanne: 35 km. west of Troyes has a 13th century church with lovely rood screen.

Chateaux in the Aube

(Tel. prefix 25)

Arcis sur Aube: 35 km. north of Troyes, 1731 chateau in park of 7 hectares. Visits with notice beforehand. Tel. 37 83 39.

Barberey St. Sulpice: 8 km. north west of Troyes. Chateau pure style Louis XIII built in brick and stone in 1626 with formal French style park. Tel. 73 36 13.

Brienne le Chateau: Military academy, covered Halle, Hotel de Ville and hospital.

Dampierre: 15 km. north west of Brienne. 16–17th century chateau, vaulted kitchens, park.

Ervy le Chatel: 40 km. south west of Troyes. Town gates, towers, ramparts, covered Halle.

Fouchères: 25 km. south west of Troyes. 18th century chateau de Vaux.

Isle Aumont: 8 km. south east of Troyes, 13th century keep, remains of chateau of Duke of Aumont. Tel. 41 81 94.

Menois: 6 km. south east of Troyes, 18th century chateau in 48 hectares, parks. Tel. 82 45 13.

La Motte Tilly: 6 km. south west of Nogent, brick chateau built 1755, park. Tel. 39 84 54.

Polisy: 35 km. south west of Bar sur Aube, chateau built 1545, huge wine pressoir.

Rumilly les Vaudes: 30 km. south east of Troyes, 16th century manor house franked by towers. Tel. 40 92 14.

Troyes: town mansions: Camusat, Chapelaines, Vauluisant, Dautruy, Deheurles, Jouvenel des Ursins, Marisy, Mauroy.

Villehardouin (val d'Auzon): 6 km. west of Brienne, keep moats, park.

Vendeuvre sur Barse: 20 km. west of Bar sur Aube, 12th century chateau, towers, keep.

Villemereuil: 10 km. south of Troyes, Louis XIII chateau, two pavilions. Tel. 41 81 36.

Villages and towns with half-timbered medieval houses

— *Brienne le Chateau*
— *Ervy le Chatel*
— *Lesmont*
— *Nogent sur Seine*
— *Ramerupt*
— *Troyes* (a score)

Museums

Arsonnal: 6 km. north west of Bar sur Aube, Musèe Municipal with collection of Russian and Byzantine icons, paintings, engravings. Closed July and Tuesdays. Tel. 26 12 54.

Brienne la Vieille: 3 km. south of Brienne le Chateau. Local artisanal agricultural museums. Guided visits from Mairie. Tel. 92 85 65.

Brienne le Chateau: Museum Napoleon Buonaparte (closed Mondays). Museum Aviation International, 60 vintage planes (weekends only).

Essoyes: 30 km. south west of Bar sur Aube. Maison de la Vigne et Vigneron, c/o Mairie. Tel. 29 60 47.

Mussy sur Seine: 40 km. south west of Bar sur Aube, Musèe de la Resistance & Maquis, rue Boursault (weekends only). Tel. 38 42 05.

Nogent sur Seine: Musée Municipale (archeology, paintings). Tel. 39 75 55.

Piney: 30 km. north east of Troyes. Maison du Parc museum.

Les Riceys: 40 km. south west of Bar sur Aube, Musée des Vieux Tacots (vintage cars), Garage Fournier, Les Riceys Bas. Tel. 29 31 53. Open Sunday afternoons.

St. Leger près Troyes: 8 km. south west of Troyes, Musée Ferme Rustique, rue de la Joncière (old fashioned farm equipment). Open Sunday afternoons. Tel. 41 72 52.

Troyes:
— Musée des Beaux Arts (natural history, archeology), 21 rue Christien de Troyes, in the abbey of St. Loup. Medieval

137

sculptures, 15th century paintings. Tel. 73 49 49. Entry fee 10 francs.

— Pharmacie Musée de l'Hotel Dieu le Comte, Quai des Comtes de Champagne. Tel. 49 55 33. Entry fee 10 francs.

— Musée Historique de Troyes et de la Champagne and Musée de la Bonneterie (textiles), unique in France, in the Hotel de Valuisant, rue de Valuisant. Tel. 73 49 49. Entry fee 10 francs.

— Maison de l'Outil, Hotel de Mauroy, 10 rue de la Trinité. Tel. 73 28 26. Collection of skilled artisans' tools for wood, leather and stone working. Entry fee 10 francs.

— Musée d'Art Moderne (collection Pierre et Denise Levy), Place St. Pierre (next to cathedral). Tel. 80 57 30. One of the best 19th and 20th century museums of modern art in France — 2,000 items — paintings, sculptures, engravings, ceramics, glass, crystals, art negre, etc. Guided visit 10 francs.

— Musée Marguerite Bourgeois, Maison Notre Dame en l'Isle, 8 rue de l'Isle. Tel. 80 54 96. Life and work of a modern day saint.

Note: museums in Troyes close on Tuesdays. A cheaper linked ticket can be purchased from the Tourist Office to reduce the entry fees payable.

Archeological sites

— *Bar sur Aube*
— *Bercenay en Othe*
— *Brienne la Vieille*
— *Estissac*
— *Nogent sur Seine*
— *Piney*

Natural wonders in the Aube

Dolmens, menhirs and polissoirs are to be found mainly in the area around Nogent. La Pierre Aigue at Resson; la Grand Pierre at la Chapelle Godefroy; la Pierre au Coq at

Transcault. Others at Bercenay, Marcilly le Hayer, Soligny les Etangs, St. Loup de Buffigny and La Saulsotte. This is one of the richest regions in France for megalithic monuments, with Celtic remains such as sanctuaries, necropolis and pottery kilns etc.

CHAPTER FIFTEEN:
THE AUBE: FOOD AND BOARD

As in Chapter Twelve, the restaurants selected afford good value with a prix fixe menu in the region of 50–60 francs per head, excluding wine. The specialities may be in the prix fixe menu or à la carte.

Ailleville: M. Bechata (N19)

Arcis sur Aube: Le Saint Hubert, 2 rue de la Marine (Rognons de veau Dijonaise, Terrine de volaille aux cèpes)

Arsonnal: La Petite Auberge (N19)

Bar sur Aube: L'Oasis

Bar sur Seine: Le Commerce, Place de la Republique

Bayel: Le Cheval Blanc; La Renaissance

Breviandes (St. Julien les Villas): Le Pan de Bois, 35 Avenue General Leclerc (N71) (Grillades au feu de bois, Tarte tatin)

Brevonnes (Piney): Le Vieux Logis (Mignardise de volaille champenoise, Filet de lotte braisé au vin des Riceys)

Clerey: L'Escapade, 27 rue de Bourgogne (Coq au Vin)

Colombey les Deux Eglises: La Montagne; Les Dhuits; Chez Janine

Lignol le Chateau: C. Aubriot (N19)

Magny Fouchard: L. Betrouin; Paul Fruschini.

Mailly le Camp: Le Saint Eloi, 5 rue de Chalons (N77) (Truite aux amandes, Lapin à la moutarde)

Montgueux (Sainte Savine): Auberge Champenoise, rue de Moulin (Rognons de veau à la crême, Escalope de saumon frais à l'oseille)

Montieramey (Lusigny sur Barse): La Mangeoire (N19); Le Menilot (Maxi brochette des Templiers, Saumon mariné aux herbes)

Nogent sur Aube (Ramerupt): L'Assiette Champenoise (Salade gourmande du Perigord, Ecrevisses à la nage)

Nogent sur Seine: Auberge du Cygne de la Crois, 22 rue des Ponts (Terrines maison, Soufflé glacé à la menthe). Le Beau Rivage, 20 rue Villiers aux Choux (Truite de la Vanne en crépinettes, Mousse au chocolat blanc et au Grand Marnier)

Proverville: Vieilhomme, rue Principale

Soulaines Dhuys: Restaurant Demongeot

Trannes: Relais de Gue

Troyes: Le Saint Vincent, Cour de la Gare (Tournedos des Vignerons, Filet de Barbue au Chablis). Au Chateaubriand, 31 rue Voltaire (Cuisse de lapin aux noisettes Foret d'Othe, Saint Jacques au champagne). Le Provencal, 18 rue General Saussier (excellent value, wide menu, good service). Tartatout 1 Cours Mertier d'Or. Le Bouffon, 25 rue Jaillant Deschainets (Escalope viennoise)

Vendoeuvre sur Barse: Le Commerce (Terrine Maison, Saumon de Fontaine à l'emince de concombre)

Villenauxe: Restaurant du Chateau; La Gare; Boule d'Or.

Hotels

Tel. (prefix 25)

Arsonval 10250	: La Chaumière (N19)	26 11 02 R
Bar sur Aube 10200:	Chalet, 55 rue General de Gaulle	27 13 74
	La Pomme d'Or, Faubourg de Belfort	27 09 93
	Le Commerce, 38 Route Nationale	29 86 36 R
Bar sur Seine 10100:	Le Commerce, 30 rue de la Republique	29 86 36 R
Brevonnes 10220	Piney: Le Vieux Logis	46 30 17 R
Brienne la Vieille		
10500:	Le Briennois, Grande Rue	92 83 71 —
Brienne le Chateau:	Le Croix Blanche, Av. Pasteur	77 80 27 R
10500	Voyageurs	n.a.
	Soleil Luisant	n.a.
	La Gaité	n.a.
Champignol:	Au Rendezvous des Voyageurs	26 42 01 R
10290		

141

La Chapelle St. Luc:	Hotel de Fouchy, 20 rue A. Briand	80 30 19 R
Clairvaux:	de l'Abbaye	26 20 12 R
Dolancourt:	Le Moulin du Landion	26 12 17 R
Fouchères 10260:	St. Parres les Vaudes,	
	Relais des Touristes (N71)	40 71 11 R
Lignol le Chateau:	Les Quatres Vents	92 04 20 R
Mailly le Camp 10230:	L'Europe, 106 rue General de Gaulle	37 30 14 R
	Le Saint Eloi, 5 rue de Chalons	37 30 04 R
	Le Centre, 64 rue General de Gaulle	37 30 08 R
Mesnil Sellières		
10220 Piney:	La Chef des Champs, Grande Rue	80 65 62 R
Montieramey 10270:	Lusigny sur Barse, Relais Paris-Basle (N19)	41 26 97 R
	Auberge de la Metairie	41 25 66 R
Mussy sur Seine:	La Commerce	38 40 37 R
Nogent sur Seine		
10400:	Le Beau Rivage, 20 rue Villiers aux Chout	39 84 27 R
	Cygne de la Croix, 22 rue des Ponts	39 91 26 R
Romilly sur Seine		
101000:	La Boule d'Or, 66 rue la Boule d'Or	24 77 48 —
	Le Palladium, 25 Place de la Gare	24 85 55 —
	Climats de France, Avenue Diderot	24 92 40 R
La Rothière 10500:	Brienne le Chateau: Auberge de la Plaine	92 21 79 R
Souligny 10320:	Bouilly: Au Relais de Montaigu,	
	300 rue Martez	40 20 20 R
St. Benoist sur Seine:	St. Benoist, Route de Mery	45 61 35 R
Troyes 10000:	Nevers, 46 rue Roger Salengro	73 36 32 —
	Paris, 54 rue Roger Salengro	73 11 70 —
	Le France, 18 Quai Dampierre	73 11 95 —
	Le Marigny, 3 rue Charbonnet	73 10 67 —
	La Mascotte, 8 rue de Preize	80 96 49 R
	du Theatre, 35 rue Jules Lebocey	73 18 47 R
	Le Trianon, 2 rue Pithou	73 18 52 R
	La Gare, 8 Boulevard Camot	78 22 84 R
	Grammont, 7 Boulevard Victor Hugo	73 22 53 —
Villenauxe:	Chateau	21 31 66
10450	La Gare	21 31 11
	Boule d'Or	21 31 63

Camp sites — Municipal
Tel. (prefix 25)

Aix en Othe 10160:	46 70 42
Arcis sur Aube 10700:	37 98 79

Bar sur Aube 10200:	27 12 94
Bar sur Seine 10110:	29 86 38
Brienne la Vieille 10500: Brienne le Chateau	92 80 31
Dienville 10500:	92 23 47
Essoyes 10360:	29 60 57
Estissac 10190, CM c/o Mairie	40 41 43
Fontaine 10200: Bar sur Aube	27 13 31
Geraudot 10220: Piney	41 24 36
Lesmont 10500: Brienne le Chateau	92 45 32
Les Riceys 10340:	29 30 32
Lusigny sur Barse 10270:	41 20 01
Marcilly le Hayer 10290:	21 74 34
Mery sur Seine 10170: c/o Mairie	n.a.
Mesnil Saint Pere 10140: (3 sites)	41 27 15
Mussy sur Seine 10250: c/o Mairie	38 40 10
Nogent sur Seine 10400:	39 76 67
Pont sur Seine 10400: (Nogent) c/o Mairie	39 84 22
Romilly sur Seine 10100: (2 sites)	24 76 60
St. Hilaire sous Romilly 10100: (Romilly)	25 51 60
St. Remy sous Barbuise 10140	37 50 95
Trainel 10400: (Nogent)	39 13 36
Troyes 10000:	81 02 64
Villeret 10330: Chavanges	92 12 68

Prices range from 1.10 francs at Essoyes to 12 francs at St. Hilaire sous Romilly. The Aube is full of countryside 'camping-caravanage' sites and their prices are very modest indeed. No less than fourteen of the sites above charge 4 francs *or less* per adult per day.

Gîtes

The Gîtes de France, 2 bis rue Jeanne d'Arc, BP 4080, 10014 Troyes, Cedex, tel. 25 73 25 36, produce a booklet each year giving details of the Chambres d'Hôtes (bed and breakfast), Camping à la Ferme, the Fermes Auberges and the Gîtes Communaux. There are over 70 gîtes available. The July and August rates are usually 50% higher than 'hors saison', i.e. the other ten months of the year.

CHAPTER SIXTEEN: NOTABLE TOWNS AND VILLAGES IN THE HAUTE MARNE

The departement (Michelin Maps 61 and 62) is an oval shape with a landmass of 6,200 sq. km. and a population of 210,000. It is heavily wooded with valleys and rivers. The Marne, the Aube and the Meuse all start their life in the Haute Marne. The departement of the Aube is to the west side and the Marne to the north. In the 250,000 hectares of woodland, wild game is abundant. The departement has a part share in the huge lake of Der-Chantecoq (see Chapter Twenty-Three).

Around Langres there are four large man-made lakes called Villegusien, la Mouche, Charmes and La Liez, reservoirs created in the 19th century for the canal of the Marne à la Saone. Fishing and all inland nautical sports, plus great walks on the Grandes Randonnées and riding, make the departement ideal for a peaceful family holiday in the green countryside.

Archeological sites abound — dolmens at la Pierre Alot, menhirs at la Haute Borne and tumuli in many villages. Gallo-Roman finds and digs are to be found at Andilly en Bassigny, Colmier le Bas, Braux le Chatel, Langres and Bourbonne les Bains.

The two oldest churches pre-AD 1050 are at Vignory and Montier en Der. The abbey of Auberive and romanesque churches with clocktowers are to be seen at Voillecomte, Ceffonds and Wassy. The cathedral of Langres is a good example of Clunisian architecture. Chateaux are to be found at Chateauvillain, Wassy, Chaumont, Joinville, Cirey sur Blaise and le Pailly.

Langres is the equivalent of Troyes, a city with classic religious, civil and military architecture with its late medieval buildings, churches and ramparts. The Aube had its bonneterie

144

(textile trade) and the Haute Marne has its coutelleries (cutlery making) mainly at Nogent en Bassigny, and chemicals and metallurgy in St. Dizier.

The three main towns for reference in this chapter are Chaumont, the prefecture city (population 30,000) in the centre on the River Marne; St. Dizier (population 40,000) in the north on the River Marne and Langres (population 12,500) in the south, also on the same river. The distances are 60 km. between St. Dizier and Chaumont, 30 km. between Chaumont and Langres.

Chaumont

Chaumont is on a steep slope overlooking the valley of the Marne and the valley of the Suize. The original chateau was built in the 10th century to dominate the two river valleys and the Counts of Champagne lived in it from AD 1228 to 1329. In the Middle Ages the tanning industry was developed and a substantial quarter known as the Faubourg des Tanneries exists on the north side.

The road from Troyes and Bar sur Aube, the N19, comes in to Chaumont from the north west. The N67 from St. Dizier from the north, N74 from Bourbonne les Bains from the north east and the N19 heads south to Langres 35 km. and Dijon. On the west side of the town the railway comes over an impressive 19th century viaduct, 300 metres long and 52 metres high.

The treaty of Chaumont was signed in 1814 by Austria, Russia, England and Prussia — a treaty of alliance for four disparate countries to link in common pursuit of Napoleon until he would be forced to quit his throne.

The Prussians occupied the town in 1871. One remembers the famous siege of Paris but forgets how much of French territory was occupied. Chaumont suffered German bombardments in 1940 and again in 1944.

In the centre of the town on the hillside are a number of 15th — 18th century houses with five gateways and towers. The 10th century keep of the castle, ramparts, the Hotel de Ville, the Fountain of Bouchardon plus the 13th century

145

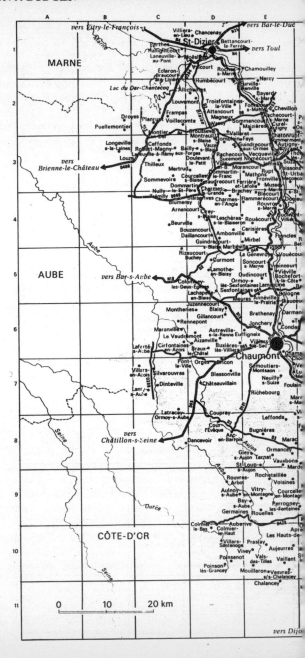

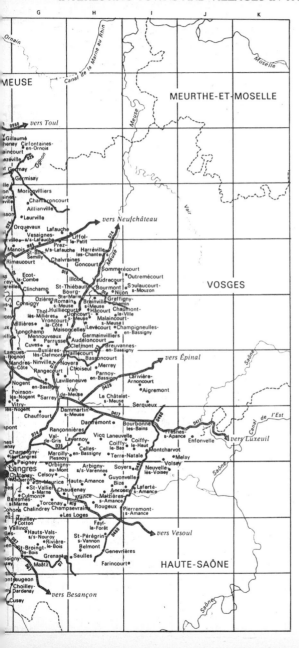

Basilica of St. Jean Baptiste and several listed churches make Chaumont an interesting town as a base for tours in central Haute Marne.

The tourist office, who are very helpful, are in the Place du General de Gaulle, opposite the railway and bus stations. They will arrange special tours of the neighbouring forests on Wednesday mornings (tel. 25 03 80 80). You can also rent a bicycle for any of ten selected circuits of varying lengths, from 25 km. (½ day) to 100 km. (2 days) or a mixture of cycling and walking. Their slogan is 'la Haute Marne, un departement mal connu à decouvrir et pourquoi pas à velo? This is a large green, pastoral, wooded unspoilt countryside *almost totally unknown to British travellers*!

Guided tours of Chaumont take place every Wednesday from 5.00 p.m. and take two hours to see the Basilique St. Jean Baptiste (and its polychromed sepulchre), the Donjon keep and the towered town mansion. Chaumont is twinned with Ashton under Lyne and there is an active committee 'de Jumelage' c/o The Mairie, 2 rue George Clemenceau. There are five modest hotels including Le Saint Jean, Le Relais, Le Royal and Le Grand Val. At the latter's restaurant they specialise in salade imperiale and andouillette marchand de vin. The buffet de la gare has a good menu too.

There are several dozen interesting little villages clustered around Chaumont — all within 'velo' distance (Michelin Map 61). In the north west section the two main roads are the N67 due north and the N19, which are crossed by the D44 and the D40 laterally from Colombey les Deux Eglises to Vignory.

The N67 runs parallel to the Marne and the Saone. Brethenay was part of Queen Mary Stuart's French dowry given in 1667 to a Jesuit college. There is a small river port with a dam on the canal Marne à la Saone. The church of Notre Dame de l'Assumption is listed.

Five km. north is Bologne (population 2,200) with a listed castle and church. The lake of Anneville is 3 km. to the west. Try the hotel/restaurant Le Commerce in Bologne.

Six km. north is Vignory which was a fortified village in the 13th century. The church of St. Etienne (see next chapter) is one of the most interesting in the departement. The hotel/

restaurant l'Etoile will give you a good meal. Eight km. north are Gudmont Villiers (16th century chateau) and Donjeux with a listed chateau and 13th century church overlooking the canal.

West of Vignory on the D40 is the forest de l'Etoile on the south side and Cerisières on the north side near Mont Gimont, known for its goat cheese.

Cirey sur Blaise, 5 km. north on the D2 has two Roman encampments and an excellent chateau mainly 17th century but part 12th century, where Voltaire stayed for many years in the period 1733–1749, as did King Charles X. In the park are deer and wild boar (see next chapter) — well worth a visit.

The D2 takes one back to **Colombey les Deux Eglises,** mainly covered in the chapter on the Aube as it is on the frontier with both departements. Nearly a million visitors come here each year to pay their respects. The church of Notre Dame en son Assumption is mainly 12th century with a lovely choir, statues and vaulted absides. A reasonable hotel/restaurant here is la Montagne.

At Rizacourt Buchey just north is the only Champagne village in the Haute Marne. There are two alternatives now — back to Chaumont on the N19 via Juzennecourt which has a chateau and La Vieille Auberge hotel-restaurant and then to Jonchery which has the hotel/restaurant l'Orée de Champagne and into Chaumont. The alternative route is to take the D23 south from Colombey through the forest of Dhuits and D15 to Rennepont (just to the west is Longchamp sur Aujon and Clairvaux abbey remains). Maranville, Cirfontaines en Azois which in pre-phyloxera days was a renowned vineyard and Pont la Ville, over the autoroute A26 to Chateauvillain (population 1,600) which has part of the 11th century ramparts standing and many listed buildings including the Hotel de Ville and the church of Notre Dame with 14th century clocktower. A local speciality is tripes à la tomate. What are Heinz and Campbells missing?

To the west of Chateauvillain are Dinteville, a listed 16th century chateau in its own parks, Lanty sur Aube with the 17th century chateau des Bussy Rabutin, Villars en Azois and Silvarouvres where about AD 630 four English Christians

149

returning from Rome to spread the gospel in England were martyred. Their names were Felix, Anglebert, Fabien and Sylvain.

The D65 is 21 km. away from Chaumont, with the airport on the south side. On the north side Braux le Chatel has a Gallo-Roman fountain and listed church of St. Anthony. Bricon was destroyed by the Germans in 1871. Villiers le Sec, which the peaceful Swedes destroyed in 1636–7, past the viaduct into Chaumont.

The north east circuit (Michelin Map 62) covers the triangle formed by the N65 signed for Neufchatel (which is just outside Champagne country), from St. Blin south east on the D16 to Bourmont and south on the D74 to Clefmont, Mortigny le Roi and back to Chaumont on the D417 via Nogent.

Andelot Blancheville is 22 km. out from Chaumont on the N65. In AD 587 a peace treaty was signed here between Gontran of Burgundy and Childebert of Austrasie. The Swedes destroyed the fortress of Monteclain in AD 1630. Many significant archeological finds have been made here including a megalith and the dolmen of Septfontaines. The abbey of that name, founded in 1223 and the Gothic 13th century church of St. Louvent, are both listed buildings.

At Manois is the 13th century church of St. Blaise and the fountain of that name where the saint performed miracles (a long time ago). At St. Blin Semilly the Swedes were here again, laying waste in AD 1636. The church of St. Martin has a 15th century fortified clocktower.

South east of Rimaucourt is the hamlet Ecot la Combe founded by a Scots mercenary in the Middle Ages (see the Abbey de la Crete). Bourmont was the home town of the Goncourt family who founded the literary Prix Goncourt. The village is on a hill and many of the old houses are listed, including the Maison Renaissance of the 16th century. So too is the church and the cheese made at nearby Illoud.

Clefmont on the D74 was known in the 11th century as Clarus Mons. Both the 11th century chateau with keep towers and ramparts and the romanesque church of St. Thiebault are listed. The four English saints stayed at Noyes, a small hamlet 'chez Dame Rictrude' before they were slaughtered in the forest of Silvarouvre. The Fountains of St. Hilaire cured rheumatism sufferers.

Nogent en Bassigny (population 5,300) is on the D1, 3 km. south of the D417. The town was taken twice by the English troops in the Hundred Years War. There are many Gallo-Roman coins, statues, remains and finds, also an Iron Age necropolis and dolmen 'la Pierre Tournante' in the forest of Marsois. It has three small chateaux and a listed church. It is a major cutlery centre and the workshops can be visited. A pilgrimage takes place on Easter Monday to the chapel of Odival. The local mineral water is very healthy. Try it at the hotel/restaurant le Commerce. Then back on the D417 to Chaumont.

On the southern circuit, south on the D101, is Semoutiers Montsaon where Tsar Alexander reviewed his victorious troops with manoeuvres in 1815, to Rickebourg, Arc en Barrois (population 1,000) where there are remains of the Roman fortress of Lamotte, a Cistercian abbey, built in AD 1119, of Longlay. Joan of Arc's father Jean was born here. The chateau, its park and the gothic church of St. Martin are all listed. A pilgrimage takes place on the 8th September to the chapel and sacred fountain of Notre Dame de Montrot.

Just 6 km. east north east is Leffonds on the D102 just to the east of the autoroute A26. The abbey of Mormant was built in the 12–13th century and is now listed. The Knights Templar of Malta owned the village for centuries (Leffonds = la fontaine in local argot). The local cheese is 'fromage de Langres'.

East to Rolamport (population 1,700) which was stormed by the English troops in AD 1435 who destroyed the chateau. The Knights Templar owned the place for several hundred years up to the Revolution. The town is on the canal of la Marne à la Saone and the 1764 bridge Pont Pregibert is listed. Nearby is the curious 'cascade petrifiante de la Tuffiere'. A local speciality is 'tarte au fromage blanc — le guerreu'.

Louvières is due north on the east side of the river and canal. The medieval church is named after St. Thomas à Beckett of Canterbury. Back on the N10 is Foulain, on the canal. On Easter Monday there is a town Easter Egg Hunt (official). The hotel/restaurant le Chalet will give you a good meal. At Luzy sur Marne which the English captured in the Hundred Years War, is the listed 13th century church of St. Gal.

Two km. north is Verbiesles where General Pershing installed his army headquarters from 1917–19 in the remains of the St. Augustin abbey founded in AD 1210. The chateau of Val des Escholiers is listed.

There is a small airport near Brottes and Chamarandes Choignes on the east bank of the river was a Protestant Huguenot centre for 150 years until the Revolution of the Edict of Nantes in 1685. The Wurtemburgers (Prussians) defeated the Imperial Guard here at Choignes, 2 km. north east on the river bank. The hotel/restaurant Au Rendezvous des Amis is in Charmarandes. And so back to Chaumont.

St. Dizier

St. Dizier (population 39,000) is the largest town in the departement and it is now industrialised. Underneath lies the Gallo-Roman stronghold of Olonne. The Christians who escaped the massacre of Langres in AD 264 took refuge with the relics of the St. Dizier. The chateau was captured by the English troops in AD 1407. A fire in 1775 destroyed much of the town and more damage was caused by the Russian troops' occupation in early 1814. Bonaparte chased them out in January, back they came and he chased them out again in March.

Since the Middle Ages the town's foundries and steel works have brought prosperity. Up to the 16th century timber was an important industry and logs were floated down the Marne which is navigable up to St. Dizier. The main roads in are the N35 from the north (Bar le Duc), N4 east from Nancy and two from the south, N67 from Chaumont (74 km.) and the D384 to Wassy and Troyes. Finally to the west is the N67 to Vitry le Francois and Paris. In the centre of town the church of St. Martin of the 12th century is listed and there are several half-timbered 16th century town houses. There is a reasonable museum, nearby airport, a theatre and several budget hotels including Le Commerce and Le Picardy. The best value restaurants are la Gare and les Voyageurs and the Bar de l'Est.

St. Dizier makes a good centre for local excursions. In particular to the south west to the huge Lac de Der Chantecoq (see Chapter 22) on the D384 past Valcourt, Moeslains, where Bonaparte beat the Russians, to Eclaron (population 2,200), once a fortified town owned by the Counts of Champagne. The 16th century flamboyant Gothic style church is listed, as is the Braucourt church. There is a huge sugar beet distillery here.

The D384 continues south west to Braucourt, Frampas to Montier en Der (population 2,400). The Benedictine abbey of Notre Dame was built here in AD 673 by St. Berchaire in the forest of Der which gave its name to the town (Monastere du Der). Despite the English army ravages in the Hundred Years War, the abbey continued to become more prosperous owning 21 villages and getting the rents from 84! The abbey is one of the major ecclesiastic sites in the departement. Concerts are given during the summer.

Ceffonds is 2 km. to the south, and has medieval half-timbered houses and the 16th century church of St. Remi, and Louze 6.5 km. further south has a 12th century church of St. Martin in a very pretty well flowered village. Just south is the manmade Etang de Blanche Terre. All the churches in this area were founded by St. Berchaire in the 7th century probably in wood and brick before stone became more usual.

Sommevoire is east on the D182, then the D13, and was a fortified town in the 11th century. Its watch tower and Templar built church of Notre Dame are listed monuments. The sacred fountain of St. Quinin is remedial for eye sufferers. The village has seven roads and seven bridges. The village fête of St. Quinin is on the first Sunday in May.

Then to Wassy via Mertrud on the D227. A small town of 3,500 population, it was occupied by the English troops during much of the Hundred Years War. Wassy was owned by Queen Marie Stuart and her family until the Duc de Guise acquired it. On a Sunday in March 1562 the Catholic Duke encouraged his 'arquebusiers' to massacre a Huguenot church congregation which started the savage wars of religion in

France. The fête of Carnival is on the second Sunday in September.

Then to Joinville (population 5,200) via Brousseval, Valleret, Fays, Nomécourt to the D960. The River Marne forms a horseshoe and curves round Joinville on the east. The site of a 10th century fort is near the splendid Chateau du Grand Jardin built in AD 1546 and surrounded by its park (see Chapter Seventeen). The pharmacy in the old hospital of Sainte Croix built in 1567 is a listed monument as is the 12th century church of Notre Dame.

Joinville is an inland port on the River Marne but also on the canals des Moulins (there are several working windmills to see) and canal de la Marne à la Saone. The views from the original chateau over the wooded countryside and river/canal patterns makes Joinville a delightful town to visit. Try the hotel/restaurant Le Nord, or La Poste and the restaurant Le Murmont across the river at Thonnance les Moulins. (On Whit Monday there is a pilgrimage to Notre Dame des Ermites).

Back to St. Dizier by the N67. The river and canal run parallel and the minor road on the east bank has its attractions — less traffic and beautiful views for 30 km. There were substantial vineyards in the Autigny region in the pre-phylloxera era.

Fontaines sur Marne is a small village on the east bank where Gallo-Roman sites are interesting — a Roman aqueduct, a second century Gallo-Roman villa and neolithic finds such as the gigantic menhir 'Haute Borne' which is 7 metres high and 2.2 metres in width at the base. Much the same at Bayard sur Marne on the opposite bank (population 1,650). On the hills of Gorzum and Chatelet two Gallo-Roman villages have been discovered and three earlier megaliths at Prez sur Marne.

The Marne valley is a treasure trove of Roman and earlier archaeological finds. In Eurville Bienville there is a 19th century chateau with listed orangery in the surrounding park. At Chamouilley on the east bank a pre-Roman Gallic tomb was found in a chalkpit as well as cellars, rooms and hypocauste (Roman central heating) of the 1st — 4th century AD. Thus back into St. Dizier either by the D8 on the east bank or the busier N67 on the west bank.

Langres

Langres (Michelin Map 66) with a population of 12,500, is the most attractive and interesting town in the Haute Marne. The N19 from Chaumont (35 km.) and the D74 link and come in from the north and run parallel to the ramparts on the west side of the town. Then they separate, on the south side the N74 to Dijon (68 km.) and the N19 to Vesoul (75 km.).

The original Gallo-Roman town of Antemadunum was the capital of the Lingones tribe, and the town was fortified as early as the 2nd century. The astonishing thing is that despite Attila the Hun, Vandals, Normans, the Hundred Years War (the English were particularly good at sacking and pillaging towns), the wars of religion, the Swedes, the Revolutionary mobs (sorry citoyens), the Allied armies of the Prussians, Russians etc., World War I and World War II, the ramparts in the main are still standing! Over 4 km. of fortified ramparts can be visited on foot, with seven watchtowers and six town gates. From the lookout towers on a fine day one can see the Vosges, the Jura hills and the mountain peak of Mont Blanc. It stands 1,600 (over 500 metres) above sea level — the River Marne being several km. to the east.

From the south west the imposing rampart names are the *Tour Navarre* (1519, *Tour d'Orval*, Porte Neuve, Porte Bouliere, Portail des Ursulines, Porte Romane, Port de l'Hotel de Ville, *Tour de Petit Saut* (small leap), *Tour St. Jean* (1538), Porte Longe Porte (1604) and Tour Piquante on the north side, Dome and Chapelle Hopital, Cremaillere to the east and a fortified enclave la Faubourg de Sous Murs, then the Porte Henri IV, Tour Virot, the *Tour St. Ferjeux* (dates specifically from 1471), Porte des Auges and finally *Porte des Moulins* in the south east corner near the Office de Tourism.

Admittedly, the city fathers have always been proud of their city and the wall repairs and maintenance of the 19th century have not impaired the genuine military style of the 15th and 16th century. Those gates and towers underlined are particularly worth looking at. The medieval city is about 1 km. in length, 300 metres in width.

Inside the city walls are five 'Sites Inscrits', the squares of Diderot, Siegler, Hotel de Ville, St. Didier and Jenson and a

155

further seven streets — Jean Roussat, Abbé Cordier, Roger, Barbier d'Aucourt, Gambetta, St. Didier and Lambert Payen. In addition a further twenty 'hotels particuliers', private town mansions, are classified IMH (Inventory of Monuments Historiques) and the best are the Maison Renaissance (rue du Cardinal Morlot), Maison Renaissance (12 rue St. Didier), Hotel de Rose (early 16th century) and Hotel du Breuil de St. Germain (1580). The Hopital de la Charité and its 17th century chapel, and the fountain de la Grenouille (1771 frogs) are classified monuments but there are still greater splendours to come!

The 2nd century Roman Arc de Triomphe has been integrated into the walls as the Porte Romaine on the west side. The 12th century Burgundian romanesque cathedral St. Mammes and its gothic 13th century cloisters stand proudly in the centre of the old town inside the ramparts (see Chapter 19). Also note the classified churches of St. Martin (13–15th century), St. Didier and its museum, the museum du Breuil de St. Germain and outside the city walls, the church Notre Dame de Deliverance built in 1873 after the Prussian invaders left. There is a pilgrimage every time that the 24th of May falls on a Sunday!

For five centuries Langres was and is, a cutlery producing centre. The gastronomic speciality is a milky cheese, cone shaped and wrapped in laurel leaves. Ask for it at the restaurants le Diderot, le Lion d'Or or the Auberge Jeanne d'Arc. There are five small, good value hotels in Langres, listed in Chapter Twenty-One. I would recommend a stay in Langres.

There are several possible circuits out of Langres. To the north east there are the two large lakes of Charmes and la Liez. Peigney has a 15th century church and a good local cheese. Charmes has a 19th century chateau Champigny les Langres, the gothic 13th century church of St. Sebastien with a fortified clocktower and a classified 18th century wooden altar.

Val de Gris (population 2,300) is a commune where the English troops beseiged and took the castles at Changey and Neuilly in the 14th century. The Gallo-Roman sites include an aqueduct, a temple to Mercury and a villa (Charge d'Eau near Andilly). Annual pilgrimages are made to the chapels of Notre Dame du Chene and St. Pierre at Dampierre. Mink breeding, bee-keeping, good local cheeses, some local wine plus the lakes, rivers and forests make Val de Gris worth a visit.

To the east and south east of Langres between the N19 and D67 there is Balesmes sur Marne where Roman fountains and baths can be seen. The source of the River Marne is here and there are grottos in the river banks (and rocks — Sabinus is their name). The 12th century Romanesque church of Notre Dame de l'Assumption is classified. The 5,000 metre Balesmes canal tunnel links the Atlantic with the Mediterranean (so the locals tell me). Emmenthal cheese 'style Francaise' is made here too.

Chalindrey (population 3,400) is a few km. to the east. The inhabitants provided materials for the Langres tanners in the Middle Ages. In the 16–17th centuries the town was known for its sorcerers and witches! The 13th century Le Pailly chateau is one of the best in the departement — it is in the Hauts Vals sous Nouroy. The English troops in the Hundred Years War occupied the castles of Pailly and Noidant Chatenoy (see Chapter Nineteen).

A pilgrimage is made to the chapel Notre Dame des Bois on the second Sunday in September. The Balesmes underground canal channel passes *below* the local church. To the east is Champsevraine which has three minor chateaux and a listed church.

Further to the south east is Fayl Billot la Forêt (population 2,000) where the 16th century church is classified. The local basketwork craft shops are worth looking at (near the N19). Chassigny Aisey to the west on the D67 once had well known vineyards and one pathetic hectare still exists at Dommarien. The church of the Virgin is 12–13th century, as is that of St. Pierre St. Paul. The cemetery has a listed 'Lantern of the Dead' dated 1551 from the Wars of Religion. The grotto of Couverte Fontaine is near Coublanc. The trout and cream cheeses are good here.

The D67 back to Langres passes just east of Piépape, again occupied by the English in the Hundred Years War. The chateaux near Villeguisien le Lac, of Piépape and St. Michel are worth a visit. The large reservoir of Vingeanne and Villegusien, plus the canal Marne à la Saone make Villegusien the most important river port in the departement. Cohons too, was taken by the English. Indeed the whole area south of Langres was occupied by our troops for much of the Hundred Years War.

In the west and south west sectors is the Lac de Saint Cierques between Langres and the autoroute, and the Rivers Aujon, Tille and Aube. Their sources are at Perrogney les Fontaines, Vals des Tilles and Vivey.

The major attractions are Auberive on the D428 with its Maison St. Jean, the remains of an 11th century Cistercian abbey. Wild boar are bred in the game reserve here. Then at Vivey, a 17th century chateau and at Poinson les Grancey a chateau and the church of St. Leger. In the deep south Chalancey, Cusey, Isomes, Montsaugeon Prauthoy, le Vallinot, Vaux sous Aubigny and Sainte Geosmes have several things in common. They are clustered together on minor roads, they were all occupied by the English, they all have either a notable Romanesque church, a Middle Ages chateau (or both) and once had prosperous vineyards.

Bourbonne les Bains (population 3,300) is a well known lush verdant spa resort 43 km. north east from Langres and 53 km. from Chaumont on the D417. In effect the town is open for business from the 1st March to the end of November and like all French spa towns (Vichy, Vittel etc.), ranges from the winter glooms (empty) to the spring, summer and autumn delights (full to the brim). The French take their health and spa resorts very seriously. There are always signs up inside the thermal treatment buildings 'Respectez la Prescription medicale!' It will be difficult, but not impossible, to call unannounced to request a mud bath unless you have a specific doctor's written recommendation.

The name Bourbonne came from the Celtic word Borvo who was a deity in the early Gallo-Roman days. The name meant 'fountains chaude' or warm water fountains. A temple to the god Borvo (and the goddess Damona) was dedicated in this spot about 2,000 years ago. The River Borne and Apance flow through the town with hot springs (60°C) which make the spa town important for remedial work on fractures, arthritis, rheumatism and respiratory problems. The first commercial thermal baths started in 1780 and Napoleon purchased the Civic Baths in 1812. The first *military* thermal hospital was opened in 1732 and increased in size in 1785. Presumably Napoleon sent his wounded veterans to Bourbonne.

In the Casino park are Gallo-Roman pillars and statues and the 12th century Gothic church of Notre Dame is listed, as is the keep and gatehouse of the chateau. The neighbouring 12th century church and crypt at Villars St. Marcellin should be seen. Its saints' tombs date from the 7th century. The season is full of fêtes and spectacles. Folklore dances and processions, fête of the vignerons (where do they come from?), fête de muguet (lilies of the valley) and gambling at the Casino.

There are several parks — the Orfeuil with fountains, another round the chateau and a large one on the north side, Parc de Montmorency. There are over a dozen hotels to accommodate the 'curistes' as the visitors are called, all at prices well below other resorts such as Aix les Bains and Vichy. Most have their own restaurants — try the Beau Sejour or the Beau Site. The spa owners are the Cie. des Thermes, B.P. 15, 52400 Bourbonne les Bains, tel. 25 90 07 20.

In the vicinity of Bourbonne les Bains, there is the source of the River Meuse (with appropriate statutary and permanent tricolores), the lake of Mezelle and several villages of interest. Coiffy le Bas (and Haut) both occupied by the Anglo Burgundian forces in the 15th century, Laneuvelle 5 km. south east, where legend has it that the local pigs were the first animals/creatures to discover the thermal sources of Bourbonne Presumably they were Roman pigs. Anyway the tradition is that the 119 inhabitants of Laneuvelle are allowed free spa waters!

Terre Natale has listed town gate houses and the church and chapel of St. Gengoulf who was born at Varennes in the 8th century. In Marcilly Plesnoy there is the 13th century chapel of Presles with classic mural paintings and a river source (the Amance) with miraculous properties. The annual pilgrimage

159

takes place in September.

To the north is Parnoy en Bassigny where in AD 1115 our Saint Etienne (Stephen) Harding caused the abbey of Morimond to be built. It ranked as the fourth in the Citeaux hierarchy.

Summary

A week in the Haute Marne departement should include two or three days in Langres (the third day to explore the countryside), one day in St. Dizier in the north, two days in Chaumont and perhaps a day drinking the waters and gambling at the Casino of Bourbonne les Bains.

CHAPTER SEVENTEEN: HISTORIC BUILDINGS AND MUSEUMS IN THE HAUTE MARNE

Main Ecclesiastical Buildings

Langres: (tel. prefix 25)
The 12–13th century cathedral of St. Mammes was formerly the seat of one of the most powerful archbishoprics in France. It has a length of 94 metres and a height of 23 metres. Although the main front facade was restored in the 18th century there are still many artistic treasures including 14th century marble statues and 16th century tapestries of the life of the saint. The treasury and the 12th century choir and apse are the best parts. The saint came from Cappadocia in the 3rd century and preached the gospel to the wild animals in Champagne country. When the Roman Emperor Auvelian sent his guards to seek the evangelist out and martyr him, the wild beasts protected him — but only for a time and his death was gruesome. Only two galleries survive of the 13th century cloisters. The 13th century church of St. Martin which is 400 metres south of the cathedral, is also listed, as is the church of St. Didier, mainly 12th century, with its museum.

Chaumont:
The 13th century Basilica of St. John the Baptist is in the rue St. Jean. In 1474 it became a collegiate church. The 14th century wooded sculpted doors and works by the sculptor J. B. Bouchardon, and the 'Rising from the Tomb' in the inner chapel of St. Sepulchre are of note, as is the ancient chapel of the Jesuit priests built 1629–40.

Auberive (west of Langres):
The ancient abbey called Maison St. Jean is 12th century with a park and cloister. Tel. 85 03 32.

161

Bourbonne les Bains:
The 13th century Gothic church has a 14th century white marble sculpture of the 'Virgin with a Bird' made by St. Savinien of Sens. The nearby 12th century church and crypt at Villars St. Marcellin are also noteworthy.

Ceffonds (south west of St. Dizier):
The flamboyant Gothic 12–16th century church is topped by a Romanesque bell tower. The 16th century Holy Sepulchre Troyes school stained glass windows should be noted.

Colombey les Deux Eglises:
The 12th century church of Notre Dame, choir and clocktower.

Isomes (south of Langres):
This is of fortified 12th century Burgundian gothic style.

Joinville (south of St. Dizier):
The 12th century church of Notre Dame has a remarkable 16th century sepulchre. Note also the Chapel of St. Anne in the cemetery and the church of Notre Dame en sa Nativité, 13th century gothic style, 9 km. away at Blecourt.

Montier en Der (south west of St. Dizier):
The 10–12th century church of Notre Dame is part of the former 7th century abbey. Its nave was destroyed by fire in 1940 but has been rebuilt. The Gothic 13th century choir, the apsidal chapels and the ambulatory are notable.

Morimond (near Bourbonne les Bains):
Cistercian abbey and lake.

Nogent en Bassigny (south east of Chaumont):
The 12–13th century Gothic church of St. Germain has strange pre-Roman chaptals and a pieta of note.

Nully Tremilly (south west of St. Dizier):
Two listed Gothic churches of the 15th century.

Poissons (south east of St. Dizier):
The church of St. Agnan was built in 1528. The vision of St. Hubert in polychromed stone sculpted in 1611, the main doors and the 'Christ with Lions' are notable.

Puellemontier (south west of St. Dizier):
The church of the Assumption of the Virgin has stained glass

windows of 1531, a 16th century apse and the nave is 12–13th century. The choir and transept are the best features.

Rouvres Arbot (south west of Langres):
Fortified church of St. Pierre ès Liens.

Vaux sous Aubigny (south of Langres)

Vignory (north of Chaumont):
The church of St. Etienne is mainly 11th century, the nave, clocktower and 30 sculptures are an excellent example of Burgundian Romanesque art.

Wassy (south of St. Dizier):
The 12th century church of Notre Dame has a romanesque nave, Gothic facade and porches. The stained glass windows are 15th century.

Chateaux

— Baudement, Chantemerle and Escarolles Lurey have feudal keeps standing.

— Chateauvillain (south west of Chaumont): remains of 11th century fortress.

— Clefmont (east of Chaumont): 11th century keep, walls and corner towers.

— Cirey sur Blaise (north west of Chaumont): partly 12th, mainly 17th century, where Voltaire lived 1734–55, including small theatre, library, salons. Visits tel. 55 43 04.

— Cusey (south of Langres): 14th century chateau, towers and ramparts.

— Dinteville (west of Chaumont): 16th century towers, kitchen, park. Tel. 02 78 01.

— Donjeux (north of Chaumont): 1755, gardens, pigonnier.

— Ecot la Combe (north east of Chaumont): 18th century towers, dungeons, wells.

— Gudmont Villières (north of Chaumont): 16th century chateau owned by the Dukes de Guise.

— Joinville (south of St. Dizier): chateau du Grand Jardin, 1546, visit to park only.

— Nully Tremilly (south west of St. Dizier): rebuilt 1713, towers, wells, parkland.

— Le Pailly (Haute Vals sous Nouroy — south east of Langres): 13th century keep, frescoes, chimneys.

— Parnot-Parnoy en Bassigny (north west of Bourbonne): 17th century, Marshal Pelissier mementoes.

— Prangey/Prauthoy (south of Langres): courtyard, salon, park, staircases. Tel. 88 22 10.

— Romain sur Meuse (north of Bourbonne): 15th century, reconstructed in 1776.

— Le Vallinot (south west of Langres): chateau de Percey le Pautel, 12–18th century, salons, chapel, drawbridge, park. Also chateau de Longeau.

— Vivey (south west of Langres): 17th century chateau.

— Wassy (south of St. Dizier): 17thcentury towers, ramparts, gatehouses.

Museums

— Bourbonne les Bains: Musée Municipal, Hotel de Ville. Wednesday and Saturday afternoons, tel. 90 01 71.

— Breuvannes en Bassigny: Musée de l'Abbé Salmon, 2 rue du Bois, tel. 31 32 12. May — October afternoons only. Souvenirs of the Abbey of Morimond, sacred art of Bassigny.

— Chaumont: Musée Municipal, Place du Palais, tel. 03 07 20. Closed Tuesdays. Archeology, paintings, sculptures, toys and dolls, Etruscan vases, 17–18th century paintings.

— Colombey les Deux Eglises: La Boisserie, General de Gaulle's home. Closed Tuesdays.

— Dammartin sur Meuse (near Bourbonne): Frère Lambert collection, local pre-history.

— Droyes: Ferme de Berzillières, 5220 Montier en Der, tel. 04 22 52. Local farming, history, implements. April — September weekends.

— Fayl le Foret: Exposition de Vannerie, Place de la Mairie, tel. 88 63 02. July, August, September only. Basket and wickerwork. Closed Sundays.

— Joinville: Musée de l'Hopital. Medieval pharmacy, pills and potions.

— Langres: Musée de l'Hotel du Breuil de Saint Germain, 2 rue Chambrulard, tel. 85 08 05. Collection of paintings, drawings, MSS, earthenware, ivories, furniture and cutlery from Langres, mementoes of Racine and Diderot. Closed Tuesdays. Musée Saint Didier: 4 Place St. Didier, tel. 85 08 05. Closed Tuesdays. Gallo-Roman antiquities, paintings 15–19th century, natural history. Also, Langres has a superb library — more of a museum — ask at the tourist office.

— Nogent en Bassigny: cutlery exhibition, Chambre Syndicate de la Coutellerie, Place du College, tel. 31 85 20. Closed August, Mondays and weekends.

— Prez sous Lafauche, 52700 Andelot, tel. 31 57 76. Zoo de Bois Musée aux Branches. Unique collection of wooden sculptures, wooden animals. Open June — September afternoons from 3.00 p.m.

— Soulacourt sur Mouzon (30 km. north of Bourbonne): Museum of old town of La Mothe.

— Saint Dizier: Musée Municipale, Square Winston Churchill, tel.56 10 11. Closed Mondays. Geology, ornithology, local history, paintings, archaeology.

— Val de Gris (north eastof Langres): Gallo-Roman museum of Charge d'Eau.

— Villiers en Lieu (near St. Dizier): Museum of vintage cars.

Natural wonders

Le Ciel du Cerf (deer) between Leurville and Orquevaut is a huge natural depression from erosion over the years and is very picturesque. Les Lacets de Meliare near Poissons is called la 'Petite Suisse'. In the plateau round Langres are the sources of the Rivers Marne, Meuse and Aube. Rouvres Arbot

165

has the extraordinary cascade petrifante d'Estuf, Soulacourt.

Towns with medieval half-timbered houses

Langres has twenty or more and Bourbonne les Bains has three.

The old Roman roads

Baudemont, Bergeres les Vertus, Gaye Lithelles, Montmirail, St. Remy sur Broyes, Le Vezir, Bourbonne les Bains, Trannes, la Rothière, Brienne la Vieille, St. Leger, Lesmont.

Gallo-Roman sites and finds

Andilly en Bassigny, Colmier le Bas, Braux le Chatel, Langres, Bourbonne les Bains and Val de Gris.

Dolmen of Septfontaines (Andelot Blancheville), la Pierre Alot (Vitry les Nogent), Champ des Perches (Arc en Barrois). Menhirs of La Haute Borne (Fontaines sur Marne).

Tumulus at Auberive and Coupray and a necropolis at Nogent 'la Pierre Tournante'.

CHAPTER EIGHTEEN:
THE HAUTE MARNE:
FOOD AND BOARD

Restaurants

Arrigny 51290: Chez Henri

Bourbonne les Bains: Herard, 29 Grande Rue (rognons de veau Saint Louis, escalope de veau à l'Indienne). L'Agriculture, 4 Avenue du Lt. Gouby (rognons à l'Ardennaise, fillet de boeuf facon du chef). Les Lauriers Roses, Place des Bains.

Bugnières 52210: Pechiodat, tel. 02 53 09.

Ceffonds: Le Cheval Blanc.

Changey 52200: Restaurant du Lac, tel. 84 07 84

Chatillon Broue 51290: Le Pot Moret

Chaumont: Hotel de France, 25 rue Toupot. Le Grand Val, Route de Langres (salade imperiale, andouillette marchand de vin). Buffet de la Gare, Place du General de Gaulle (soufflé de saumon, canard aux pêches)

Chavanges 10330: Au Bon Acceuil

Dampierre 52360: Le Manoir, tel. 84 00 03

Droyes 52220: l'Etoile

Eclaron 52290: la Petite Auberge

Fayl Billot 52500: Bar de l'Eglise, tel. 88 67 80

Foulain 52800 (Nogent en Bassigny): Le Chalet N19 (salade de foie de volaille au vinaigre de framboise)

Joinville 52300: Restaurant de la Poste, Place de la Greve. Le Murmont, Thonnance les Joinville.

Lac de Charmes 52360: Petits Charmes, D74, tel. 84 07 81. La Forge, D74, tel. 84 07 71.

Langres 52200: Le Diderot, 4 rue de l'Estres (feuillete d'escargots, escalope de saumon rosé à la fleur de moutarde). Le Lion d'Or, Route de Vesoul (cassolette d'escargots à la creme d'ail, paupiette de plie aux asperges). La Poste, 8–10 Place Ziegler. La Bonne Auberge.

Montier en Der: Au Petit Pont, 28 rue de l'Isle. Au Joli Bois.

Montigny le Roi 52140: Le Moderne (from 68 francs), Avenue de Lierneux (salade gourmande, escalope de boeuf aux cèpes)

Nogent en Bassigny 52800: du Commerce, 51 Place Charles de Gaulle.

Saint Dizier 52100: Le Gambetta, 62 rue Gambetta (scampis frits sauce tartare, filet de canard à l'aigre doux). Le Relais des Nations, Route de Vitry (assiette des pecheur, cassolette d'escargots aux cèpes). Le Gare et les Voyageurs, 32 Avenue de Verdun (cuisse de grenouilles à la Provencale, rognons de veau flambés). Restaurant Champagne, 19 rue J. P. Timbaud (Marnaval)

St. Loup sur Aujon 52210: Aux Rives de l'Aujon, tel. 84 40 14.

Villars Santenoge 52160: Au Bon Acceuil, tel. 84 23 01.

Hotels

As in Chapters Twelve and Sixteen, the hotels selected offer double rooms for about 100 francs (for the room) with breakfast extra. (Tel. prefix 23).

		Tel. (prefix 23)
Andelot 52700,	Le Cantarel, Place Cantarel	01 31 13 R
Arc en Barrois 52210,	Hotel du Parc	02 53 07 R
Bannes 52360,	Chez Francoise les Routiers	84 08 81 R
Bologne 52310,	Le Commerces, Place de la Mairie	01 41 18 R
Bourbonne les Bains		
52400:	Le Bourgogne, 64 rue Vellonne	90 00 81 R
	Les Buissonnets, 20 rue Vellone	90 08 76 —
	Herard, 20 Grande Rue	90 13 33 R
	Les Lauriers Roses, Place des Bains	90 00 97 R
	L'Agriculture, 4 Avenue de Lt. Gouby	90 00 25 R
	Les Bains, 25 rue d'Orfeuil	90 05 71 R

	Beau Sejour, 17 rue d'Orfeuil	90 00 34 R
	Beau Site, 21 rue de la Chavanne	90 04 25 R
	A l'Etoile d'Or, 55 Grande Place	90 06 05 R
Chamarandes		
Choignes 52000	Chaumont, Au Rendezvous des Amis	03 20 16 R
Chaudenay 52600	Chalindrey, No Man's Land (!)	84 95 23 R
Chaumont 52000:	Hotel de France, 25 rue Toupot	03 01 11 R
	Le Royal, 31 rue Mareschal	03 01 08 —
	Le Grand Val, Route de Langres	03 90 35 R
Colombey les Deux		
Eglises 52330,	La Montagne	01 51 69 R
Condes 52000,	La Chaumière (N67)	03 03 84 R
Eclaron 52290,	Hotel de la Cloche	04 11 17 R
Fayl Billot 52500,	Hotel du Cheval Blanc, Place la Barre	88 61 44 R
Foulain 52800	Nogent, Le Chalet (N19)	31 11 11 R
Giffaumont 51290,	Le Cheval Blanc du Lac	72 62 65 R
Joinville 52300,	Le Nord, 1 rue Camille Gillet	96 10 97 R
Jonchery 52000,	L'Oree de Champagne (N19)	32 30 84 R
Juzennecourt 52330,	La Vieille Auberge	07 53 02 R
Langres 52200:	Le Cheval Blanc, 4 rue de l'Estres	87 07 00 R
	Grand Hotel de l'Europe, 23 rue Diderot	87 10 88 R
	Le Lion d'Or, Route de Vesoul	87 03 30 R
	Les Moulins, 5 Place Etats Unis	87 08 12 R
	La Poste, 8 Place Ziegler	87 10 51 —
Longeau 52250:	Hotel de l'Escale	88 42 59 R
	Cafe des Routiers (RN)	88 40 51 R
Marnay sur Marne		
52800,	La Vallée (N19)	31 10 11 R
Montier en Der 52220:	Auberge de Puisie	04 23 18 R
	Hotel le Dervois, Route de Wassy	04 22 76 R
Montigny le Roi		
52140,	Val de Meuse, Aux Sources de la Meuse	90 30 09 R
Neuilly l'Eveque		
52360,	Hotel de Bourgogne	84 00 36 R
Nogent en Bassigny		
52800:	Le Chalet (N19)	31 11 11 R
	du Commerce, 51 Place Charles de Gaulle	31 81 14 R
Peigney 52200,	Langres, Auberge des Voilliers, Lac la Liez	87 05 74 R
Rouvres Arbot 52190,	Hotel Guido	84 23 74 R
Saint Dizier 52100,	La Gare et des Voyageurs, 32 Ave. Verdun	05 01 25 R
	Le Commerce, 3 Place Aristide Briand	05 20 96 —
	Le Picardy, 15 Avenue Verdun	05 09 12 —

Villegusien le Lac		
52190,	La Charmille	88 46 88 R
Vivey 52160,	Relais du Lys	84 81 01 R

Camp sites — Municipal, in the Haute Marne

Tel. (prefix 25)

Andelot Blancheville 52700	01 91 35
Arc en Barrois 52210	02 53 11
Auberive 52160 c/o Mairie	n.a.
Bannes 52360 Neuilly l'Eveque	85 24 55
Blaiserives 52110	55 43 75
Bourbonne les Bains 52400	90 08 64
Bourg 52200 Langres c/o Mairie	87 03 32
Braucourt 52290 Eclaron	04 13 20
Chatonrupt 52300 Joinville	95 11 82
Chaumont 52000	32 11 98
Coiffy le Haut 52400 Bourbonne les Bains	90 01 38
Eclaron 52290	04 11 05
Humes Jorquenay 52200 Langres	87 50 65
Joinville 52300	96 06 64
Langres 52200 c/o Mairie	87 03 32
Montigny le Roi 52140 Val de Meuse, c/o Mairie	90 31 50
Peigney 52200 Langres	87 00 33
Poissons 52230 c/o Mairie	n.a.
St. Ciergues 52200 Langres, c/o Mairie	n.a.
Villegusien le Lac 52190 Prauthoy	88 47 25
Vovecourt 52320 Froncies	02 42 21
Wassy 52136 c/o Mairie	55 31 90

Campsite prices per adult per day range from Wassy 2.60 francs and Chatonrupt 2.75 francs, to Breaucourt at 11 francs; less than 14 of the sites above charge 4 francs or *less* per adult per day.

The Gîtes headquarters is at 1 rue du Commandant Hugueny, B.P. 509, 52011 Chaumont, tel. 32 88 88. Over 125 gîtes, fermes, auberges and gîtes d'etapes are available. High season rates are about 500–700 francs per family per week and 25–30% less out of season.

CHAPTER NINETEEN:
SPORT AND LEISURE ACTIVITIES

Canal holidays

To hire a cruising boat the best place to contact is Bateau Ecole (Monsieur A. Heitz), 7 Boulevard Paul Doumer, 51100 Reims, tel. 26 47 03 58. There are six local government information points where advice on local rents will be given. They are called Service de la Navigation.

1. 76 rue de Talleyrand, 51084 Reims, tel. 26 40 36 42.
2. Pavillon de la Navigation, BP 403, 51308 Vitry le Francois, tel. 26 74 18 99.
3. Arrondissement Fonctionnel, 82 rue Cdt. du Hugueny, 52011 Chaumont, tel. 25 32 53 33.
4. Subdivision de Langres, 2 rue Robert Schuman, 52200 Langres, tel. 25 87 02 94.
5. Chemin de Barrage, BP 256, 51011 Chalons sur Marne, tel. 26 65 17 42.
6. Subdivision Mixte de Saint Dizier, Chausée Saint Thiebault 52100 Saint Dizier, tel. 25 05 03 17.

The rivers/canals, 600 km. of them, flow from south to north from Burgundy between the four lakes around Langres on the canal de la Marne à la Saone, past Chaumont, north to St. Dizier past the huge Lac du Der Chantecoq to Vitry le Francois, on the canal Internal à la Marne to Chalons sur Marne, Epernay and via the canal de l'Aisne à la Marne past Reims to Berry au Bac, Rethel,Autigny in the Ardennes.
The five 'fluvial' routes are more specifically:

1. Canal de la Marne à la Saone. From Vitry le Francois calling at 30 towns and villages before reaching Cusey — or vice versa!

2. Canal de l'Aisne à la Marne. From Loivre and four other ports of call to Conde sur Marne.
3. La Marne. From Dormans, Port à Binson, Damery to Epernay.
4. Canal Internal à la Marne. From Dizy and 12 ports to Vitry le Francois.
5. Canal de la Marne au Rhin. From Vitry le Francois and two ports to Sermaize les Bains.

UK companies offering boating holidays in Champagne include Blakes Enterprise, French Country and Renaissance. If you wish to join an existing cruise there are several local possibilities.

1. Champagne Air Show, 15 Bis, Place St. Nicaise, 51100 Reims, tel. 26 82 59 60.
2. Mlle. Grandhomme, Coche d'Eau, rue du Petit Parc, 51300 Vitry le Francois, tel. 26 74 05 85.
3. In the UK, Blueline Cruisers, P.O. Box 9, Hayling Island, PO11 0NL, tel. 0705 468011.
4. Centre Sportif-U-Folep, Giffaumont 51290, St. Remy en Bouzemont, tel. 26 72 63 57.

Charges vary but the latter's tariff is 150 francs per person per day, plus 15 francs per petit dejeuner and stop for lunch at local port auberge.

Canoe/kayak holidays

Any of the villages on the following rivers will be a good base for such a holiday. The Blaise, la Saulx, le Rognon and l'Aire but also on the major rivers of the Marne and Aube.

Sailing/windsurfing/swimming

The four lakes around Langres — Charmes 200 hectares, Liez 270 hectares, Monche 94 hectares and Villegusien 200 hectares — are all ideal. So too is the huge Der Chantecoq of 4,800 hectares based on Vitry le Francois or Giffaumont Champaubert, 51290 St. Remy en Bouzement, tel. 26 41 62 80 and the Lac du Foret d'Orient based on Troyes, tel. 25 41

21 64. Each lake has villages in which you can stay and rent boats and windsurfing equipment.

Horse-riding

The local tourist offices and Syndicat d'Initiative will advise you of the whereabouts of the nearest riding stables. Alternatively, you can write direct to Tourisme Equestre (Acate), 22 rue du Parades, 51220 St. Thierry, tel. 26 49 00 11 for all local 'centres equestres'. In the Aube there are centres at Chaource, Brienne la Vieille and Lusigny sur Barse. In the Haute Marne at Arc en Barrois, St. Dizier and Changey.

Walking

The French long-distance public footpaths on a national basis are well signed and easy to 'read'. The GR2 crosses the Pays d'Othe for 148 km. The GR24 starts at Bar sur Seine, through the natural regional park of the Forest d'Orient through the woods, vineyards and cultivated plains for 141 km. There are offshoots — the GR24A (50 km.), GR24B (57 km.), GR24C (24 km.) and GR24D. The GR12 is a branch of the European GR3 (Atlantic Bohemian) but this is mainly in the Ardennes departement. The GR14 is perhaps the most topical. With its variations GR141 follows the Montagne de Reims through the vineyards, through Champagne to Bar le Duc. Detailed Topoguides are available in the UK from McCarta Limited, 122 Kings Cross Road, London WC1.

Fishing

The tourist offices and Syndicat d'Initiative will advise you of the local regulations. Generally a temporary permit or licence is required which costs very little. You may need to join the local fishing club or association as a temporary member. Also write to Monsieur Philippe Lhure, St. Just Sauvage, 51260 Anglure, tel. 26 80 01 10.

Ballooning

Called montgolfières, they can be booked from Champagne Air Show, 15 Bis, Place St. Nicaise, 51100 Reims, tel. 26 82 59 60 for flights between April and October.

Cycling

Many SNCF stations such as Saint Ménéhould have a renting facility. The Cyclists Touring Club, 69 Mead Row, Godalming, Surrey GU7 3HS provides an information sheet on French facilities to its members. Ask at your local French tourist office in Champagne.

Golf

There are two 18 hole and four 9 hole courses. The former are Golf de Reims, Chateau des Dames de France, 51390 Guelx, tel. 26 03 60 14; Golf du Chateau de la Cordelière, 10210 Chaource, tel. 25 40 11 05.

Visiting 'Parcs Floraux'

There are five open to the public:

— Le Petit Jard, 51000 Chalons sur Marne
— Pepinieres et Arboretum St. Anthoine, 10130 Ervy le Chatel, tel. 25 70 50 33
— Parc Floral de Menois, 10800 Rouilly St. Loup (near Troyes), tel. 25 82 45 13
— Jardin d'Horticulture P. Scneiter, Boulevard Roederer, 51000 Reims
— Arboretum de Montmorency, 52400 Bourbonne les Bains

Animal parks (i.e. not zoos)

Parc Animalier de la Bannie, 52400 Bourbonne les Bains and Enclos de vision de gibier (wild game) de Montavoir, 52160 Auberive. The former has 250 acres with wild boar, fallow deer, stags and wild sheep and an aviary. The latter near Etuf petrified waterfall has three parks. One for fallow deer, another for roe deer and the last for wild boar.

Ornithological reserves

Lac du Der Chantecoq, Giffaumont Champaubert 51290 St. Remy en Bouzemont and Lac de la Foret d'Orient, 10220 Piney.

Visits to the villages fleuris

Villages which have won the annual competition for the best gardens and floral borders in the whole of France. Baconnes (Marne) 4 fleurs, Haussimont (Marne) 4 fleurs and Vitry le Francois (Marne) 1 fleur.

The most picturesque village

Recently the award went to Coiffy le Haut, 4 km. from Bourbonne les Bains. Amongst other things, a new vineyard has been replanted on the old vineyard slopes of the Middle Ages.

Bored children?

Take them to Nigoland open air fun and adventure park at Dolancourt Bar sur Aube, tel. 25 26 14 54, just off N19 east of Troyes.

Nature study/botany

Branta Travel, 11 Uxbridge Street, London W8 7TQ, tel. 01 229 7231 run specialist holidays to the Champagne area.

Tennis

Every town and most of the larger villages in Champagne have one or more public courts — ask at the tourist office. In the holiday centres around the half dozen large lakes there are many public courts.

Art appreciation

Swan Hellenic Art Treasures Tours, 77 New Oxford Street, London WC1A 1PP, tel. 01 831 1616 run specific tours to the Champagne area, to Reims, Troyes, Langres etc.

Battlefield Tours

Major and Mrs. Holt's Battlefield Tours, Golden Key Building, 15 Market Street, Sandwich, Kent CT 13 9DA, tel. 0304 612248 run tours and visits to the battlefields of the Marne.

Weekend de cuisine Champenoise

The Hotel d'Orfeuil, 29 rue d'Orfeuil, 524000 Bourbonne les Bains, tel. 25 90 05 71 will fix you up for a cost of 450 francs.

A week 'de cure detente'

A week at the spa with first class treatment and two star hotel, all meals (including 'menus basses calories' if you want them) for 1,800 francs. Hotel/restaurant de Bourgogne, 64 rue Vellonne, 52400 Bourbonne les Bains, tel. 25 90 00 81.

A cycling weekend 'au Pays des 4 lacs', 235 francs

Office de Toursime au Plateau de Langres, Place Bel Air, 52200 Langres, tel. 25 87 03 32.

To show you how helpful and efficient the local tourist offices can be, I have used Epernay as an example. Their Green Guide in three languages has details of visits to sculpture restorers, vine growers, bee keepers, angora rabbit breeders, glass engravers and painters, botanists, horticulturalists, exotic bird rearing (élévage d'oisseaux exotiques), artisans of various kinds (metal workers, textile weavers, painting on textiles), as well as more mundane information on bicycle rentals, gîtes rureaux, chambre d'hote, gîte d'etape, camping and caravanning, ferme auberge, etc. etc.

176

CHAPTER TWENTY:
THE NATIONAL PARKS AND THE GREAT LAKE

Montagne de Reims

The Montagne de Reims (Marne) lies in the zone north west of Chalons sur Marne between Reims and Epernay. The total area is 50,000 hectares (125,000 acres) of which 7,000 hectares are vineyards, 23,000 hectares agricultural land and 20,000 hectares forests. There are 33,000 people in 68 local communes living in the Park, including those around Reims and Epernay but in particular Verzy, Ay, Chatillon and Ville en Tardenois. The major hills (not mountains) are near Verzy (287 metres), Mount Sinai and Mount Joli. It is not only a major nature reserve but man's activities are also controlled. The 'quality of life' and the protection of the rural life are two of the major purposes, as well, of course, as game, flora and fauna protection from marauding man.

Look out for the honey market at Verzy and the strange twisted trees called les Faux (some of them over 500 years old) a peculiar mutation of the beech tree. Also the Maison de l'Artisan at Ville en Tardenois, the Maison de la Foret et du Bucheron at Germaine, the Ecomusée du Champagne, the Porte du Parc at Ville en Tardenois, the relais equestre at Sarcy, archery contests at Villers sous Chatillon. The Grande Randonnée GR 14 criss-crosses the Park through vineyards and forests.

The roads to take are the D26 covering the north boundary of the Park via Verzy, Verzenay (windmills), Rilly la Montagne, Montchenot, Sracy and St. Lie. The D380, D386 and D71 bisect the Park through the forests and from west to east via Ville en Tardenois, Pourcy, Nanteuil la Foret, Germaine and Louvois (chateau). At Mount Sinai there is an observatory and lovely views from St. Lié, Sarcy and Verzenay.

The main information centre is Parc Naturel Regional de la Montagne de Reims, Maison du Parc, Pourcy, 51160 Ay, tel. 26 59 44 44. Also the Bureau du Parc, 86 rue Belin, 51100 Reims, tel. 26 40 43 84.

Forest of the Orient Park

The second major park and regional nature reserve is the Forest of the Orient Park (Aube). It was created in 1970 and consists of 67,000 hectares (170,000) acres spread over 44 communes with a population of 18,000 people. The tourist office is in the Maison du Parc at Geraudot, 10220 Piney, tel. 25 45 35 57.

In the centre of the huge forest is an equally large lake of 2,500 hectares (6,250 acres) in retangular shape. It has a number of purposes, being a natural reservoir for the River Seine, fed by a canal from the south (canal d'arrivée) and in turn feeding the Seine to the west (canal de restitution).

Mesnil St. Pere

The N19 from Troyes to Chaumont passes within 1 km. to the south of the lake via Lusigny sur Barse and la Villeneuve au Chene. Minor roads, the D1, D28, D43, skirt the lake linking up the small villages of Mesnil St. Pere, la Loge aux Chevres and Geraudot. The former is the naval base with a swimming beach and several sailing schools. The latter has a notable 12–16th century church and a good beach. There is an animal park of 80 hectares with wild game in the forest of Piney on a large headland north east of the lake. It overlooks a large ornithological reserve for water fowl with an observatory (between Geraudot and the Maison du Parc). Thousands of migrating birds arrive punctually twice a year coming and going to and from the north to Africa.

There are camping facilities at Mesnil St. Pere, tel. 25 41 27 15 and at Géraudot, tel. 25 41 24 36. For visiting fishermen the Association is at 10/12 rue Francois Gentil, Troyes, tel. 25 73 35 82. Guided tours are made from Port de Mesnil, St. Pere. Bookings at the Societé Ondine de l'Orient, 10 rue de Côte d'Or, 10140 Vendeuvre sur Barse, tel. 25 41 21 64. From March — July and the boat trips take one hour.

Weekend tours

Two weekend planned visits and tours are also possible. One from the Office de Tourisme de Troyes, 16 Boulevard Carnot, tel. 25 73 00 36 and the other is a bicycling tour organised by the hotel/restaurant le Vieux Logis, Brevonnes 10220 Piney, tel. 25 46 30 17 which includes for two people, two rented bikes, two picnic lunches, maps, two evening meals and a double room, total 537 francs. Try also La Mangeoire, N19, 10270 Le Menilot, tel. 25 41 20 72.

Lake of Der Chantecoq

The Lake of Der Chantecoq is the largest man-made reservoir in France with nearly 5,000 hectares (12,500 acres) of water. It is situated south west of St. Dizier D384, south east of Vitry le Francois D13, and north of Montier en Der. It was created in 1974 to regularise the course of the River Marne and the lake is fed by a canal from the north east corner and feeds out into the Marne from a canal in the north west corner. Three villages were totally submerged, Champaubert aux Bois, Chantecoq and Nuisement aux Bois. Only the churches survived and were rebuilt at Sainte Marie du Lac on the D560 on the north side. The lake has a shore periphery of 77 km. of which 19 are embankments.

The three pleasure ports are at Giffaumont Champaubert on the south side, Nemours on the north east side and Sainte Marie du Lac Nuisement on the north side. There are six plages (beaches) and at the Port de Chantecoq on the west side there is water ski-ing, motor boats and sailing. On the eastern side one can fish (perch and trout), ride, walk or see the local artisans at work. There is a village museum at Sainte Marie. Guided boat tours on the lake leave from Giffaumont,

179

Office de Tourisme du Lac du Der Chantecoq, 51290 St. Remy en Bouzemont, tel. 26 41 62 80.

Migrating birds, ducks and herons have their reserved places on the west side at l'Argentolle and the east at the Reservoir de Champaubert. Bicycles for hire at Giffaumont and les Bouchots. Camping facilities at five sites around the lake.

There are four local hotel/restaurants nearby:

— The Cheval Blanc du Lac, 51290 Giffaumont, tel. 26 72 62 65. Menus from 55 francs

— Le Cheval Blanc, 52220 Ceffonds, tel. 25 04 20 46. Menus from 45 francs

— Hotel de la Cloche, 52290 Eclaron, tel. 25 04 11 17. Menus from 42 francs

— La Bocagere Auberge, 51290 Sainte Marie du Lac, tel. 26 72 37 40

For the young in heart there are discos at Sainte Livière and Larzicourt. At Montier en Der to the south one can visit Le Haras National with never less than 35 stallions. Guided visits of one hour, tel. 25 04 22 17. At Berzillières, just south of Giffaumont, is the Musée Agricole with over 400 vintage farm machines and instruments, tel. 25 04 22 52. Monsieur Fagot will show you la Grange aux Abeilles (apiary and exhibition of exotic insects including scorpions), tel. 26 72 61 97.

The Association Touristique des Amis du Lac, 51290 Sainte Marie du Lac, tel. 26 72 36 46, help ensure the preservation and protection of the game reserves and run the village museum.

CHAPTER TWENTY-ONE: INFORMATION AND USEFUL ADDRESSES

The main tourist offices in the three departements are as below:

Aube   Tel.

1. Association Departementale de Tourisme,
   Hotel du Departement, BP 394, 10026 Troyes, Cedex   25 73 48 01
2. Office de Tourisme, 16 Boulevard Carnot, 1000 Troyes 25 40 42 18
3. Office de Tourisme, 24 Quai Dampierre, 1000 Troyes   25 73 36 88
4. Pisciculture de la Vanne, 10190 Estissac   25 40 42 18
5. Acceuil en Milieu Rural Aubois, Chambre d'Agriculture,
   2 Bis, rue Jeanne d'Arc, BP 4080, 10014 Troyes   25 73 25 36
6. Comité de Tourisme du Barsequannais, Mairie,
   Bar sur Aube   25 38 80 35
7. Comité de Tourisme du Pays d'Othe, Mairie, Estissac   25 40 41 43
8. Comité de Tourisme Nogentais, 33 rue du Poncelot,
   10400 Nogent   25 25 83 68
9. Confrérie des Vignerons Aubois, 10300 Montgueux   25 74 84 60
10. Club Nautique Aubois, Hotel de Ville, 1000 Troyes   25 43 52 57

Marne

1. Comité Departemental de Tourisme de la Marne,
   2 Bis, Boulevard Vaubecourt, 51000 Chalons sur Marne 25 68 37 52
2. Offices de Tourisme:
   51000 Chalons sur Marne, 3 Quai des Arts   26 65 17 89
   51700 Dormains, rue du Port   26 58 21 45
   51200 Epernay, 7 Avenue de Champagne   26 55 33 00
   51170 Fismes, 28 rue René Letilly   26 78 05 50
   51290 Lac du Der Chantecoq, St. Remy en Bouzemont,
   Maison du Lac   26 47 25 69
   51100 Reims, 1 rue Jadart   26 47 25 69
   51800 Sainte Ménéhould, Place du General Leclerc   26 60 85 83

51300 Vitry le Francois, Place Giraud	26 74 45 30
51120 Sezanne, S.I., Place de la Republique	26 80 51 43
51700 Chatillon sur Marne, 11 rue de l'Eglise	26 58 34 66

3. Camping, Caravanning, Hotels & Restaurants: Comité Regional de Tourisme, 5 rue de Jericho, 51000 Chalons sur Marne   26 64 35 92

4. Gîtes Rureaux, Chambre d'Agriculture, Route des Suippés, BP 525, 51009 Chalons sur Marne   26 64 08 13

Haute Marne

    Tel.

1. Comité Departemental du Tourisme, 52011 Chaumont   25 32 65 00
2. Offices de Tourisme: 52400 Bourbonne les Bains,

Centre Borvo	25 90 01 71
52200 Langres, Place des Etats Unis	25 85 03 32
52100 St. Dizier, Jardin du Jard	25 05 31 84

3. Syndicats d'Initiative:

52210 Arc en Barrois, Mairie	25 02 51 33
52150 Bourmont, Mairie	25 01 16 46
52000 Chaumont, Boulevard Thiers	25 03 04 74
52300 Joinville, Mairie	25 93 16 01
52220 Montier en Der, Mairie	25 04 22 62
52140 Montigny le Roi, Mairie	25 86 11 50
52130 Wassy, Mairie	25 55 31 90

Also at Poissons, Trois Vallées and Orquevaux.

4. Chambre Syndicale de la Coutellerie, Place Charles de Gaulle, BP 12, 52800 Nogent en Bassigny (cutlery is *the* local industry)   25 31 85 20

5. Gîtes Ruraux, Hotel du Conseil General, 89 rue Victoire de la Marne, 52011 Chaumont   25 32 65 00

6. Confrerie du Taste Fromage de Langres (Monsieur Lodiot), Bay sur Aube, 52160 Auberive   25 86 23 72

7. Three local Maisons du Tourisme: One on the autoroute A31, another at the Aire de Perrogney les Fontaines and the Aire de Noidant les Rocheux. (Aires are friendly tourist halts off main roads — well signed up). Another is the Pavillon de la Haute Marne, la Croix d'Arles, Bourg 52200 Langres.

Guided visits (some free, some payable)

Aube
1. Office de Tourisme de Troyes
2. S.I. de Villenauxe la Grande, Hotel de Ville, 10370 Villenauxe la Grande, tel. 25 21 32 22

Marne
By the Tourist Offices at Chalons sur Marne, Dormans, Chatillon sur Marne, Giffaumont Champaubert (Lac), Reims, Sainte Ménéhould and Sezanne.

Haute Marne
1. Arc en Barrois
2. Bourbonne les Bains
3. Bourmont
4. Langres
5. St. Dizier

Son et lumière

The Marne is the most sophisticated with cathedrals and key monuments at Chalons sur Marne and Reims being illuminated at night. So too in Troyes (Aube) and Langres (Haute Marne).

In the Marne four other key sites are illuminated. Abbey of Trois Fontaines (Saturdays), Chateau de Braux Sainte Cohière, village museum of Sainte Marie du Lac, and the great Basilica de l'Epine.

Son et lumière manifestations are at the Chateau la Motte Tilly (Aube) in midsummer, Chateau de Vendeuvre sur Barse (Aube) in July, Cathedral Notre Dame of Reims in June — September. Basilica St. Remi in Reims ; Marne) weekends in summer; St. Amand sur Fion (Marne) in midsummer; Braux Sainte Cohière (Marne) in June — September.

The most picturesque markets

Aube

Sainte Savine	Flower market, Sunday morning
Estissac	St. Catherine's Fair on 25th November

Ardennes le Meuse à Monthermé

Marne

Sezanne	Flea markets, 1st Sunday June & September
Reims	Flea market 'au Boulingrin', 1st Sunday in September
St. Imoges	Flea market, beginning September
Chalons sur Marne	St. Martin's Fair, Saturday after 11th November
Vitry le Francois	St. Martin's Fair, 10th November

Haute Marne

Langres	St. Catherine's Fair, 25th November

Confreries

The local wine club associations — the Confreries — who are responsible for fêtes, wine dinners and general jollity are now listed.

1. Confrerie des Echevins de Bouzy, Bouzy 51150, Tours sur Marne.
2. Ordre des Côteaux de Champagne, 30 rue de Talleyrand, 51100 Reims. Tel. 26 40 16 68.
3. Confrerie de Saint Vincent de Vertus, BP13, 51130 Vertus. Tel. 26 52 10 57.
4. Confrerie Gastronomique des Compagnons du Pied d'Or, Auberge du Soleil d'Or, 2 rue Chanzy, 51800 Ste. Ménéhould. Tel. 26 60 82 49.

Bibliography

Michelin Green Guide (en francais) Champagne-Ardennes: superb on local history and architectural data on ecclesiastical buildings.

Champagne and sparkling wines by Jane McQuitty (Mitchell Beazley): detailed background on all the most important champagne houses and personalities.

Comité Interprofessionnel du Vin de Champagne, 5 rue Henry Martin, 51200 Epernay, tel. 26 54 47 20: Background data and statistics on the champagne industry.

The History of Champagne by André Simon, Octopus Books Limited.